Highest Yoga Tantra and Mahamudra

無上密與大手印

by **Sheng-yen Lu**

Translated by Cheng Yew Chung

A US Daden Culture Publication

US Daden Culture LLC
3440 Foothill Blvd.
Oakland, CA 94601
U.S.A.
Website: www.usdaden.com
Email: us.daden.culture@gmail.com

Lu, Sheng-yen, 1945-
Highest Yoga Tantra and Mahamudra/by Sheng-yen Lu;
translated by Cheng Yew Chung;
edited by Alice Yang and Jason Yu;
proofread by Jacky Ho and Dance Smith.

Library of Congress Control Number(PCN): 2012938871
ISBN-13: 978-0-9841561-6-0
1. True Buddha School. 2. Chinese-Tantrayana Buddhism.
Cover design and layout by US Daden Culture Design Team
Photograph by US Daden Culture
Set in Minion Pro 12
US Daden books are printed on acid-free paper and meet the guidelines for the permanence and durability set by the Council of Library Resources.

Printed in U.S.A.

ISBN 978-0-9841561-6-0
51200>

9 780984 156160

Special Acknowledgements

The True Buddha Translation Teams (TBTTs) would like to express the highest honor and deepest gratitude to Living Buddha Lian-sheng, Sheng-yen Lu, and Master Lianxiang for their continuing support and guidance on the translation effort. Without their compassion, wisdom, blessings, and encouragement, this project would not have reached fruition.

In addition, we would like to acknowledge the diligent work put forth by the following volunteers on this project: Cheng Yew Chung (translator), Alice Yang and Jason Yu (editors), Jacky Ho and Dance Smith (proofreaders), Renee Cordsen (desk-top publication) and Gia Tran (quality control). We would like to thank these dedicated and selfless volunteers who have contributed their time and effort to promote the works of Living Buddha Lian-sheng, and to support the publications of US Daden Culture.

We would also like to extend our sincere appreciation to all other volunteers who work behind the scenes, facilitating the translation process, and handling administrative responsibilities.

May all volunteers be blessed for their immeasurable merits. May all sentient beings benefit from the ocean of wisdom.

Table of Contents

The Highest Yoga Tantra and Mahamudra are profound and unfathomable, but I am willing to explain the teachings using a simple language, according to my own realization and actual practice.

Sheng-yen Lu

Preface: Pith Instructions in the Anuttarayoga Tantra

After the publication of my fiftieth book, I plan to write a book detailing the pith instructions that have been secretly transmitted in the Vajrayana lineage. This book will be entitled *Highest Yoga Tantra and Mahamudra*, and the debut of this masterpiece will awaken and tremble the whole universe. As a result, Vajrayana Buddhism [a.k.a. Tantric Buddhism] will become an eternally glorious rainbow in the sky, liberating and blessing all sentient beings and heavenly beings. I will be the first in modern times to completely reveal these ancient teachings in writing. (This book shall be my fifty-first book .)

I have been secretly practicing the Highest Yoga Tantra and Mahamudra for many years, and these teachings were transmitted to me by the Sixteenth Gyalwa Karmapa and Guru Padmasambhava. Now, Master Sheng-yen Lu will unveil the closely guarded secrets of this lineage. These secrets are the supreme quintessence of Vajrayana Buddhism. They contain the extremely rare and pith instructions for all

Vajrayana practitioners to attain buddhahood. I, the Holy Red Crown Vajra Guru, am the master of the inextinguishable dharma lamp. I am the master that knows all secrets and who expounds the Highest Yoga Tantra. When this book is published, it will send shockwaves throughout the world.

In the past, Vajradhara (a secret epithet that represents the great authority of Vajrayana Buddhism) first transmitted the Highest Yoga Tantra and Mahamudra to Tilopa, who later transmitted them to Naropa. [Naropa then passed the dharma baton to Marpa], who was originally from the snow-capped mountains of Tibet. Marpa established the Kagyupa School, the white sect of Tibetan Buddhism. Marpa's successor was Milarepa, who attained buddhahood in his present body, as the result of his attainment from the Highest Yoga Tantra and Mahamudra.

When I received the secret empowerment from the Sixteenth Gyalwa Karmapa, His Holiness conferred the teachings of the Highest Yoga Tantra and Mahamudra to me. He also entrusted me with the responsibility of propagating the principal teachings of attaining buddhahood to everyone, when the time was ripe for Vajrayana to blossom in the world. When I received this transmission, I vowed to offer my entire body and mind to all buddhas of the ten directions, transforming myself into hundreds and thousands of bodies. I vowed to be continually reborn in order to liberate sentient beings from the great ocean of samsara.

The lineages I received come from a mix of different traditions and lineages, which include the following:

The Red Sect/Nyingma School - bestowal of the empowerment of the Great Perfection of the Nyingma School in my meditation.

The White Sect/Kagyu School - bestowal of the secret transmission by His Holiness the Sixteenth Gyalwa Karmapa and the Twelfth Tai Situpa Rinpoche, Pema Donyo Nyinje Wangpo.

The Yellow Sect/Gelug School - bestowal of the empowerment

from Guru Thubten Dargye.

The Flower Sect/Sakya School - bestowal of the great empowerment from Sakya Zhengkong Lama. In the Zongchi Temple, Guru Pufang gave me Cundi Bodhisattva Empowerment.

About one thousand year ago, the lineage holder Marpa validated the Highest Yoga Tantra and Mahamudra after practicing diligently for eighteen years in India. It then took Milarepa [Marpa's disciple] twelve years to practice the pith instructions, in the White Horse Tooth Cave of the high mountains of Tibet. Milarepa was able to achieve yogic union through Mahamudra, and achieved all supernatural faculties. Among the yogic practitioners of the Kagyu lineage, Milarepa was among the most famous and highly accomplished.

The Highest Yoga Tantra and Mahamudra are profound and unfathomable, but I am willing to explain the teachings using a simple language, according to my own realization and actual practice. This will help readers to understand the secret instructions. It is extremely challenging to write this kind of book. Therefore, the completion of this book relies on the protection of Vajradhara. The spiritual energy naturally released from this book can illuminate the sentient beings of the ten directions, and allow all beings to receive blessings.

The Highest Tantra Yoga and Mahamudra literally mean "great union." These teachings are the heart essence of attaining buddhahood. They completely penetrate and reveal the reality of the self-nature. Through yogic practices, one achieves union with buddhas and the self-nature. Therefore, they are the most incredible secret practices in the world and are known as the Middle Way Vajrayana. They are non-dual, are neither empty nor existing, but are always residing perfectly in the middle way. When the practitioner attains the middle way, he attains nirvana, and therefore is not bound to continual rebirth. Instead, he resides freely in a state of no birth and no death.

The practices of the Highest Yoga Tantra and Mahamudra involve the purification of the body, speech and mind, which are the common practices of the Three Secrets. The practices also include the wonderfully subtle Pith Instructions of Insight, the Pith Instructions of Tranquility, the Method of Breathing, and the Vase Body Method, which are supreme Tantric treasures. They are truly priceless. Whoever practices the Highest Yoga Tantra and Mahamudra will be endowed with incredible peace and joy, and will know the secrets of the heavens and the physical realms. He will attain buddhahood in the present body. Thus, the secret for attaining buddhahood is contained in the teachings of Highest Tantra Yoga, which were once lost and hidden for countless centuries.

One time when I was deeply absorbed in meditation, practicing the Highest Yoga Tantra and Mahamudra, I met and paid homage to Mahasiddhi Saraha, Nagarjuna, Lama Kazi Dawa Samdup, Marpa, Arapati, Milarepa, and more than a hundred others. I prostrated to the lineage holders of the teachings, and in return they praised and encouraged the Holy Red Crown Vajra Guru. The lineage holders believed that Master Lian-sheng's dedicated practice qualified him to be a genuine Tantric master, one who could deliver countless sentient beings to enter the path to enlightenment. Through actual practice, I have gained realization and achieved great dharma power. The formidable vow that I made stems from the strength of vows made throughout many lifetimes. The lineage holders praised this great dharma affinity that had never been encountered in the past. The number of sentient beings that would be liberated by Master Lian-sheng would be as vast as the stars in the sky, and limitless like the grains of sand in the Ganges.

In my deep meditation I experienced supreme joy, and during deep absorption I was filled with such happiness that tears flowed from my eyes. When I first mentioned to my guru that I would write a book about the Highest Yoga Tantra and Mahamudra, my guru said, "These teachings are considered extremely precious by the lineage holders. Therefore, the teachings can only be revealed publicly after seeking permission from one's guru. If you wish to reveal these teachings, you must first seek permission from the lineage holders during your meditation."

Thus, I entered into deep meditation to seek permission from the lineage holders. The lineage holders said:

> The revelations of the Highest Yoga Tantra and Mahamudra are linked to the great causes and conditions of Master Lian-sheng bringing the Dharma from the East to the West. There is extraordinary spiritual significance to these revelations. Today, through the pen of Master Lian-sheng, the teachings shall be made available to all those who eagerly seek the great teachings, paving a path for them to follow. That is the secret within the secrets. The teachings that are about to be disclosed are a mandate from heaven. This unveiling will be a great dharma event of the current times, and it has been destined to take place since time immemorial. If one wishes to practice the Highest Yoga Tantra and Mahamudra, one must be guided by a genuine master who can confer the empowerment, and clarify and expound on any unclear parts. No one should practice this teaching blindly and follow only the printed materials. These wonderful teachings are made known to help sentient beings understand their contents, and appreciate their profoundness and supremeness. Hence, sentient beings should quickly find a suitable master to take refuge in, and focus wholeheartedly on this affinity. They should practice truthfully to attain realization. For the above reasons, the affinity of this great Dharma has ripened.

My fifty-first book will address the topics of vidya (knowledge of enlightenment), adhyatma vidya (inner studies), and anuttarayoga (Highest Yoga Tantra). I named this book the *Highest Yoga Tantra and Mahamudra* because it possesses the sacred teachings of mind purification. Since I have attained fruition in these teachings, I vowed that I would propagate them. The teachings of the Highest Yoga Tantra and Mahamudra are like the rising sun that transforms all darkness into a brilliant world. I have reached the attainment of a throne holder, and my debating skills are sharp and persuasive. I have destroyed the illusionary mara and I have attained the unexcelled yoga, just like the Victorious Lion King did. These great teachings shall be propagated throughout the world for time immemorial.

I have been secretly cultivating for more than ten years. The secret to my success lies in the fact that no matter where I am, whether it is at home or whether I'm traveling, entertaining guests, ill, bedridden with sickness, disturbed by mara, working, exhausted, encountering calamities and so forth, I have never once abandoned my daily cultivation. Not once did I succumb to laziness nor indulge in rest. My unending perseverance and devotion of blood, sweat, and tears is a testimony to my achievement. This is the key strength of my cultivation and attainment. The one thing that I can say I am proud of is the fact that I have been practicing earnestly. There is nothing to be proud of except for the fact that in the last ten years or more, I have never once missed my daily cultivation.

The teachings of the *Highest Yoga Tantra and Mahamudra* will soon be published, and the darkness that shrouds the world will disappear at once. Buddhas and bodhisattvas have fulfilled our wishes by reaching out their compassionate hands. The most valuable Tantric teachings, which are all-encompassing and perfect, will soon be presented to all sentient beings. Followers of the different traditions of Vajrayana Buddhism and those with the proper dharma affinities to read this book, shall be blessed by the guru and attain great spiritual power. This book will connect all sentient beings of the ten directions, allowing them equally to achieve spiritual accomplishments.

May 1984, True Buddha Attic, Seattle
Preface by Holy Red Crown Vajra Guru, Sheng-yen Lu.

1. Homage to the Lineage Holders of Mahamudra

Can you guess how long I have been practicing the Vajrayana Buddhism for in secret? To be honest, if the readers are paying attention, the hint about my experiences in Tantric cultivation can be found on line 1 of page 3 in my first [Chinese] spiritual book, *Encounters with the World of Spirits*. This [Chinese] book has been published for more than ten years. Thus, I have been practicing Vajrayana Buddhism for at least ten years.

Readers who come across this book, *Highest Yoga Tantra and Mahamudra,* have great affinity because it contains the most supreme Tantric Dharma in the world. It was secretly guarded and was not supposed to be taught openly. Now that you are able to read it, you are definitely blessed with immense affinity. Therefore, you must first pay homage and express gratitude to all lineage holders of the supreme meditative Mahamudra. Let us prostrate to the lineage holders in the heavenly realms!

In ancient India, during the Song Dynasty (988 - 1069 CE), the primordial buddha, Vajradhara, transmitted Mahamudra to Tilopa. Tilopa then passed the lineage to Naropa. From Naropa, the line was handed to Marpa, then to Milarepa, Gampopa, Karmapa and so forth. The pith teachings of the meditative Mahamudra were transmitted by these lineage holders

In modern times, His Holiness the Sixteenth Gyalwa Karmapa (1924 - 1981 CE) transmitted the Mahamudra teaching to the Holy Red Crown Vajra Guru, Master Sheng-yen Lu. Now that Vajrayana has reached from the East to the West, the secret pith teachings have finally taken root in the West. As a result, students of Master Lian-sheng, Sheng-yen Lu can now receive the true lineage of Vajrayana in the West and gain the wonderful wisdom for attaining buddhahood. Hence, westerners are given the opportunity to reach the realm of liberation and be freed from samsara.

One time during deep meditation, I found myself wearing the five-buddha crown and I ascended on a jeweled-lotus throne towards the Tushita Heaven. I was accompanied by many holy sages, and upon arriving I met Maitreya Bodhisattva as well as the other lineage holders. They each pressed their palms on my forehead and urged me to take on the heavy responsibility of delivering sentient beings in the human world.

They instructed me to announce the following message: when we prostrate to the Mahamudra lineage holders, we should repent with all sincerity. It is an inconceivable meritorious act that the bodhisattvas have turned the dharma wheel to expound the proper teachings of the Highest Yoga Tantra and Mahamudra. The rare dharma affinity that represents the buddhas' great compassion has ripened. Therefore, the major Vajrayana teachings are now revealed to all sentient beings of the ten directions. One who believes in the teachings, takes refuge and cultivates this practice will have the opportunity to attain buddhahood.

The lineage holders gathered at the residence of Maitreya Bodhisattva and requested me to write a book about the vital points of Mahamudra. Meditative Mahamudra are the highest Vajrayana teachings, which are able to purify the bodies, speech and minds of sentient beings. By practicing Mahamudra, they will be able to link with the highest cosmic consciousness and unite with the ultimate nature. Thus, many sentient beings will be delivered. I shall be the first to give the comprehensive teachings of Mahamudra.

[During deep meditation,] the light of the Mirror-like Wisdom was beaming from me, and the lineage holders were seated above my head in multiple layers. At the highest position, there was Vajradhara, followed by Tilopa, Naropa, Marpa, Milarepa, Gampopa and Karmapa. Karmapa was immediately above me and I, Vajra Master Lian-sheng, was the present lineage holder. I have realized all Buddha-dharma and have attained buddhahood in this very body.

Tibetan Buddhism entered Tibet around 747 CE and honors Guru Padmasambhava as the founding teacher. During that time, when Vajrayana Buddhism entered Tibet and when Subhakarasimha, Vajrabodhi, and Amoghavajra brought Vajrayana Buddhism into China, many difficulties were encountered especially regarding language barriers that hindered communication. Thubten Dargye, my guru from the Gelug order, once told me that the essential instructions of Tibetan Buddhism were not easily available because there were too many hindrances.

Moreover, in the past, the essential instructions of Vajrayana Buddhism were passed orally from masters to students. These key points are the quintessence of Mahamudra, allowing one to attain buddhahood in this very body. Therefore, they were only transmitted within the lineage to individuals with supreme faculties. That is why the transmission of Vajrayana Buddhism was rare and not widespread. I hope that those who come across this book and wish to practice the teachings will take refuge in a guru, seek his blessings, and receive the true key points from him. Only then is it possible to assure that the practice is done accurately and guarantees that one achieves spiritual union.

In the past if one wanted to practice Vajrayana Buddhism, one had to first study the exoteric scriptures for a number of years. Then one had to pass the examinations of a Geshe to prove one's proficiency in Sutrayana, before being admitted into the Tantric monasteries. Only after that could one learn Tantric Dharma from the guru. The Vajrayana teachings are the ultimate dharma gate of Mahayana. They represent the highest order of teachings, which were hidden from the public and transmitted in secrecy between the teachers and students. This form of transmission constitutes the fundamental principle of Vajrayana Buddhism.

Now that we are in the degenerative stage of Buddha-dharma, the sublime teachings of the Three Secrets are openly propagated and revealed. Vajrayana is blossoming and the traditions of Tibetan, Chinese, and Japanese Esoteric Buddhism are becoming mainstream again. These forms are certainly not as rigid and strict as they used to be.

I received the heart essence of Mahamudra and I possessed the two authority seals. I also obtained the great secretive, perfect empowerments from the four Tantric schools of Nyingma, Gelug, Kagyu, and Sakya. As the contemporary spiritual holder of the Vajrayana Buddhism, I have been validated by gaining yogic union and have obtained the blessings of the lineage holders. I am entrusted with the responsibility of writing this book on the Highest Yoga Tantra and Mahamudra, and I will provide the pith instructions in detail without hiding or holding anything back. In this way, everyone may know these teachings and receive the benefits from them. With this book, I hope to plant the seeds of Vajrayana so that all sentient beings may be born into a family that practices Vajrayana Buddhism, whether in the present or future lifetimes.

These vital points of Mahamudra were developed by the Kagyu order, commonly known as the White Sect in Chinese Buddhist circles. Before the time of Milarepa, the lay adepts who attained buddhahood wore white clothing. Hence, they were called the White Sect. According to my knowledge, however, there is another meaning to this name. It signifies the transformation of black karma into white karma, which leads to buddhahood. This is one of the major meanings of the White Sect.

Some Tantric masters have asked me, "Master Sheng-yen Lu, who exactly are you?"

I shall herein disclose everything about myself: I was born on May 18, 1945 (lunar calendar) at noon, in Houhu, County of Jiayi. My father's name is Lu Ershun and my mother is Huang Yunu. My last name is Lu and my first name is Sheng-yen, and I was born during the midst of air strikes by Japanese warplanes. Therefore, my parents were on the run and I was born on a chicken farm. 1945 was the year of the rooster.

My religious journey led me to follow Christianity, Taoism, the Tiande Sect (Heavenly Virtue), Sutrayana, and Vajrayana Buddhism. Later, I saw that I was the emanation of White Mahapadmakumara of the Maha Twin Lotus Ponds in Sukhavati, who had returned to the human world due to my previous vows to deliver sentient beings. This is my fourth reincarnation on earth.

I practiced the respective sadhanas of the four Vajrayana schools, according to the respective transmissions of the lineage orders. In the Kagyu School, I am the forty-second lineage holder counting from Vajradhara, the seventeenth if you count from the Karmapas, and the thirty-third counting from Tilopa.

Amitabha Buddha of Sukhavati, Guru Padmasambhava, and the Karmapas all entrusted White Mahapadmakumara of the Maha Twin Lotus Ponds, with a heavy responsibility to incarnate four times on earth. These reincarnations are evidence of his great compassion. The Holy Red Crown Vajra Guru, Master Sheng-yen Lu is also the Immovable Vajra Master who is not affected by any slanders or criticism. In the future, he shall become a Buddha with the epithet, the Non-Evil

Eye Tathagata. The Maha Twin Lotus Ponds is a realm that was manifested by the Non-Evil Eye Tathagata.

I first had my spirit awakened by my teacher Lin Qiandai. Later, through various circumstances I received trainings from the invisible spirit guide, the Eminent Sanshan-Jiuhou. I cultivated according to the teachings of Taoism, Sutrayana, and Vajrayana, beginning first with Taoism, then Sutrayana and finally Vajrayana. My teachers include Lin Qiandai, Taoist Master Qingzhen, the Eminent Sanshan-Jiuhou, Venerable Yinshun, Venerable Leguo, Venerable Daoan, Venerable Huisan, Venerable Xiandun, Venerable Jueguang, Master Xiao Changming, the Sixteenth Gyalwa Karmapa, the Twelytdsssssss ssssssssssssssssssssssxnb3whg,olle,logftrfth Tai Situpa Rinpoche, Guru Pufang, Guru Thubten Dargye, Sakya Zhengkong Lama, Guru Padmasambhava and others. I have mastered the teachings of the Great Perfection, Mahamudra, Lamdre and Yamantaka Sadhana. Examples of these accomplishments include the Seven Treasures , the Mother-Child Luminosity Tantra, Clear Light Yoga, teachings of Kunga Drolchok, and sadhana on the peaceful and wrathful deities, among other practices. I received spiritual responses in all of them.

I have been endowed with the blessings of the buddhas, bodhisattvas and the power of White Mahapadmakumara through my yogic union. This profound revelation of the Highest Yoga Tantra and Mahamudra will allow sentient beings to be guided by the buddhas' light, and be empowered by the buddhas to attain buddhahood. Those who hold this book should immediately pay homage to the Mahamudra lineage holders because the emergence of this kind of dharma work is rarely seen. This book constitutes the great secret of Padmakumara's mission to ferry sentient beings to the other shore.

2. Mahamudra is a Method of Attaining Buddhahood

If my disciples practice the Highest Yoga Tantra and Mahamudra as outlined in my book, follow the teachings with accuracy, receive the guidance from a genuine master, and maintain vigorous practice, I guarantee that if they should not attain buddhahood, then I shall be held responsible.

Mahamudra is an unexcelled method of attaining buddhahood. Once an individual practices it, the ordinary mundane mind will resonate with the universal mind. In other words, you become one and inseparable with the original nature of the universe in the present body. At this time, you will be aware of your self-nature and the intrinsic nature of the universe. You will understand that you are truth itself and the truth is you, and that there is no difference between the two.

The term Mahamudra in Sanskrit or Chakgya Chenpo in Tibetan means the "Great Seal." Mahamudra is the quintessence of attaining buddhahood. This practice is also called the Middle Way, and it relies completely on training the mind with specific techniques to reach the single buddha vehicle. Upon reaching this state, one perceives the true reality behind all things. The final goal of all cultivators is to partake in the right path, resulting in the fruition of the realm of nirvana, attaining buddhahood, and freeing oneself from the bondage of cyclic existence. One will eventually attain complete spiritual freedom.

I would say that anyone who practices Mahamudra Yoga and gains attainment shall reach the state of wonderful action of the mind and spirit, in which all movements and actions reflect the cultivation and attainment of Mahamudra. Thus, one will reach the level of spontaneous expression, which is beyond the state of an ordinary mundane mortal.

I once said:

> The very act of eating is an act of offering. Offerings are made in the upper realms to the buddhas and bodhisattvas. In the middle realms, offerings are made to the devas. In the lower realms, offerings are made to the sentient beings suffering in the six realms. Therefore, the act of consuming food is just like performing the homa ritual, which is the Mahamudra practice of Mandala Offering.

> The very act of clothing oneself is an act of guarding oneself by using Armor Protection, which is called secret adornment. Hence, getting dressed is the spontaneous arising of the Mahamudra of Adornment.

> The very act of bathing is an act of cleansing one's limbs, mouth, and body. Hence, this constitutes the spontaneous emergence of the Mahamudra of Purification.

> The very act of speaking is an act of transforming all speech and sound into a mantra because all utterances are the recitation of mantra, which is the Mahamudra of Speech Purification.

> The very act of sleeping is the Yoga of Clear Light, where

the sleeping postures are in fact Mahamudra postures.

The true meaning of Mahamudra is the complete transformation of the mundane ordinary mind into a holy mind, for every desire has an antidote in Mahamudra. Thus, an ordinary person is transformed into the mind of a holy sage. All negative karma that arises from ignorance is eliminated, leaving no trace of even a single dust particle. All aspects of truth are continuously revealed and have inexhaustible meanings, which are the expression of infinite wisdom.

I would like to declare that anyone who practices Mahamudra, whether he or she is an ordained monk or a nun, or a layperson, is the one who has vowed to attain buddhahood. In this regard, he or she has accepted the transcendental method and instructions of the Highest Tantra Yoga, which should be considered as the true act of renunciation. All past practices are incomparable to the teachings of Highest Tantra Yoga and Mahamudra, which encompass all other teachings and wisdom. All other practices are eternally embodied in these supreme teachings. Thus, by practicing Mahamudra, one attains true renunciation.

When a Tantric Buddhist practitioner of the Kagyu order attains realization through the practice of Mahamudra, at that time the mundane teachings, Sutrayana teachings, dharma gates, rules and precepts, and Tantric teachings all become shattered. However, those who are not enlightened cannot understand this. Thus, I will not elucidate further on this because any explanation may immediately become a misunderstanding. This truth is only understood by one who has realized and attained buddhahood.

I am an accomplished adept because it is a supreme victory to attain buddhahood. Therefore, I have earned the status of a teacher in the human and spiritual worlds because I, an enlightened Vajra master, have demonstrated and proved the process of attaining buddhahood. My titles include the "Emanation of White Mahapadmakumara of the Maha Twin Lotus Ponds," "religious torchbearer," "one who enlightens man and succors the world," "Holy Red Crown Vajra Guru," and "Tantric Master Lian-sheng, Sheng-yen Lu." Those who follow my practices and read my books are indeed endowed with the affinity to attain buddhahood.

Those who wish to learn from me must meet the following five conditions:

The first condition is to take refuge in the Holy Red Crown Vajra Guru. Why? This is because I have spiritual attainments from actual cultivation, and I know the Vajrayana Buddhism for attaining buddhahood. I am the Buddha and the Buddha is me. There is really no difference. I know the means to deliver sentient beings, and those who follow my methods shall reach buddhahood. I am the representative of the holy Sangha, and I am a holy Sangha member myself. I represent the unification of the Guru, Buddha, Dharma and Sangha. Therefore, I embody the Triple Jewels. Thus, taking refuge in the Holy Red Crown Vajra Guru is equivalent to taking refuge in the Buddha, Dharma, and Sangha. To practice Buddha-dharma, we must follow the rules of studying Buddhism. Upon taking refuge, one develops faith. Those without faith and who haven't taken refuge will find it impossible to enter the Vajrayana path. Without the guru's power of blessings and responses, there will be no accomplishment.

The second condition is generating the bodhicitta. This vow refers to perseverance in cultivation, with the intention of attaining buddhahood and delivering sentient beings. It is expressed through the Four Immeasurable Vows, which are: "May all beings have happiness and the causes of happiness. This is Immeasurable Loving-kindness. May all beings be free from suffering and the causes of suffering. This is Immeasurable Compassion. May all beings live in eternal peace and delight, without suffering. This is Immeasurable Joy. May all beings abide in equanimity, and be free from attraction and aversion. This is Immeasurable Equanimity." I want my students motivated towards reaching buddhahood and to cultivate diligently and consistently, in order to build a solid foundation. Upon reaching buddha-hood, one must vow to return to deliver sentient beings so that all may attain the fruition of buddhahood. This is the highest aspiration.

The third condition is repentance. Not only do the speech and actions of ordinary beings generate negative karma, but their discursive thoughts also do as well. Hence, the behavior of ordinary beings is distorted, confused, illusory, and entwined with negative karma. Before starting any practice, humans are subject to the influence of the defiled mind and are unaware of the purified mind of self-nature. They are affected by afflictions, impulsiveness, and obstacles. Thus, they are really miserable. The *Sutra on the Eight Realizations* states, "The mind is the source of evil, while the form is the assembly of crimes." One whose body and mind are drowning in a deep pool of transgressions is completely unaware of his or her predicament. Therefore, it is necessary to repent and cultivate the Four Preliminaries, especially the Vajrasattva Practice, also known as the Vajrasattva Hundred-Syllable Mantra Practice. Through the recitation of the Hundred Syllable Mantra, negative karma is eliminated.

The fourth condition is to make offerings to the guru. Since the guru is the embodiment of the Triple Jewels, making offerings to the guru is equivalent to making offerings to the Buddha, Dharma, and Sangha. A true guru who accepts the offerings from his disciples does not delight in these donations, but rather he uses this wealth as a means to benefit sentient beings through the completion of his duties and assignments. Through your offerings, the guru may help to reduce your karma and bless you. The act of making offerings constitutes the path of generosity, and can carry the meaning of renunciation from worldly affairs and samsara. When one makes offerings to the guru, one receives his blessings and naturally gains spiritual responses quickly.

The fifth condition is to swiftly attain spiritual union with the guru. Those who follow my teachings must first practice Guru Yoga.

One should know that the yogic power from the lineage gurus is the only secret to attaining buddhahood. Guru Yoga is the first Dharma gate that one practices in attaining buddhahood through Mahamudra. One must recite the Guru Mantra: *Om ah hum guru-bei ah-ha-sa-sa-ma-ha lian-sheng siddhi hum*. Form the Padmakumara Mudra where the right hand forms the Teaching Mudra, and the left hand forms the Lotus Holding Mudra. Visualize the lineage holders seated in meditation and arranged in levels according to the order of transmission. At the top level there is Vajradhara, and at the lowest level there is Guru Lian-sheng. The lineage holders emit a spectrum of light that enters into the practitioner's body. The initial step in gaining the wisdom of Mahamudra lies in obtaining responses in Guru Yoga. The key secret of this uncommon teaching is the active supplication of the lineage holders to bestow their guidance and blessings. In this way one becomes close with the gurus and receives their transmission.

It is only upon fulfilling these five conditions that one truly becomes my lineage disciple.

Mahamudra is the method of attaining buddhahood. By revealing this major practice and its secrets, many senior leaders of Vajrayana Buddhism around the world will most likely be astonished. The world shall witness the re-emergence of this major teaching that has only been transmitted in secrecy in past generations. The key instructions of Master Sheng-yen Lu come from a long line of gurus. With the publication of this book, the teachings shall continue to be transmitted into the future, so that everyone will be able to partake in its precious secrets. Take note, however, that we must practice in gradual steps, beginning with the fulfillment of the five conditions. We must then practice the Four Preliminaries, followed by Guru Yoga, Personal Deity Yoga, the Vajra Practices, and finally the Highest Yoga Tantra. Before one can cultivate the Mahamudra, one must gain realization through these stages.

Thus this book is precious and extraordinary, and it should be treasured. I would like to once again emphasize that the true teaching of actual practice is the Mahamudra of attaining buddhahood.

Mahamudra involves the practice of winds, channels, and light drops. This is the approach for attaining buddhahood in this very body. It is not an empty theory.

Sheng-yen Lu

3. Meditation of Vairocana

In Mahamudra, we must first learn the seven-point meditation posture, which is also known as the seven-point posture of Vairocana. This meditation posture is intended to balance the mind and body through the seated posture. In India, the sitting meditation posture is called the full-lotus position, and we know it as the crossed-legged position. As it is often seen in Buddhist statues, the legs are depicted in the vajra posture, with both legs crossed and the soles facing upwards. This is why it is called the vajra position.

By sitting in the full-lotus position, the body and mind are completely balanced, discursive thoughts are removed, and blood circulation is improved. The body is able to remain soft, yet it also able to endure discomfort. Moreover, through the seven-point meditation posture, one can obtain the primordial wisdom, achieve meditational stability, and directly attain buddhahood.

Why is it called the seven-point posture of Vairocana? It is because Vairocana Buddha, the Great Sun Tathagata, is the central Buddha of the Five Dhyani Buddhas and the principal deity of Esoteric Buddhism. Being the main deity in both the Vajradhatu Mandala and

Garbhadhatu Mandala, his status and position symbolize universal luminosity.

Forming the Wisdom-Fist Mudra [Bodhyagri Mudra], Vairocana presides over the Vajradhatu or Diamond Mandala as the "Vairocana Wisdom Dharmakaya." In the Garbhadhatu or Womb Mandala, he displays the Dharmadhatu Mudra and is called "Vairocana of Reasons Dharmakaya."

According to the Buddhist scriptures, the image of Vairocana is described as follows:

> The golden-colored Vairocana is enthroned on an eight-petaled lotus. Appearing as a bodhisattva, he is seated cross-legged on a jeweled lotus. He wears a five-buddha crown decorated with white sashes. Behind him, there is a five-colored halo with a round aura on top. He emanates rays of magnificent and vibrant lights from his entire body, and he has dark maroon hair that falls to his shoulders. Vairocana is adorned with glittering earrings and attired with tiers of precious jewels, blue pearls, and ornaments that fall down to his knees. He wears jade or pearl armlets on his arms, and golden bracelets on his wrists. Vairocana's hands are crossed with the palms facing upwards. The right hand rests on the left hand with two thumbs touching each other. He places this mudra beneath the navel and enters into meditative absorption. He also wears a thin layer of white celestial clothing, a skirt made of multiple textiles such as blue brocade and silk, and a green sash wrapped around his waist.

The inner merits of Vairocana represent the bright dharma realm of suchness, and the outer merits represent the illumination of all sentient beings without hindrances. These merits are perfect, constant, and unchanged. The merits also embody the Buddha-nature of all sentient beings and buddhas, so the brilliance of the merits is omnipresent. It is called the "Light of s Tathagata," which equally illuminates all dharma realms.

Vairocana is always sitting and is never seen in a standing posture. This carries a deeper meaning. Since he is the central figure of the Dhyani Buddhas, he is depicted in images as entering into profound deep meditation. Thus, the teachings of Mahamudra begin with the meditation posture of Vairocana, where the legs are crossed in the full-lotus position and the soles of the feet face upwards.

Some who have short legs or stiff joints may find it impossible to cross their legs and form the full-lotus position. However, they should at least attempt to adjust their soles to face upwards and pull their legs towards the body to achieve a balanced posture.

The hands form the Dharmadhatu Mudra with palms facing upwards, resting beneath the navel point. The right hand is placed over the left hand. One may form an alternate mudra with the tip of the middle fingers touching each other and the thumbs placed at the lower portion of the index fingers. We can use either of these two mudras, so long as the mudra that we form is consistent.

Keep the chest up and slightly move the shoulders backwards. The chin is slightly tucked in, just like a soldier would raise his chest and tuck his chin in during training.

Press the tongue lightly against the upper palate. This is of vital importance. Taoists refer to this as "bridging heaven and earth" or "building a celestial bridge." When animals go into hibernation, they also rest with their tongues touching the upper palate. When a practitioner first practices Mahamudra, he will not be able to enter into true tranquility if his tongue does not touch his upper palate. In India, the act of pressing the tongue against the upper palate is called khechari. Aside from touching the tongue to the upper roof of the palate, the tongue must also be rolled far backwards towards the throat (slipping behind the nasopharynx) and press against either nasal opening. In this way, one achieves the balance between body and mind, and the disruptive flow of breath is calmed. Through this method, one's lifespan can be extended and one's essence is kept in place without depletion. By pressing the tongue against the upper palate, the tongue must also curl like a hook, which is then placed against the inner nostril. The Taoist views the tongue as a bridge between one's shen or spirit that resides in the head, and one's body and heart.

The next aspect of Vairocana meditation is the act of gazing at an object. Even though most Mahamudra practitioners sit cross-legged in the lotus posture, form the mudra beneath the navel (resting on the lap), lift their chests, and press the tongue against the upper palate, their minds may still wander and generate discursive thoughts. Thus, when we want to pacify our mind, we must first focus on one point. One begins training by taking an object, placing it within five and a half feet of one's gaze, and concentrating on it without letting the gaze waver. In time, one should be able to gaze longer and once the focus becomes fixed, the mind will stabilize. Without focus, the mind will wander. When the mind drifts away, the gaze will lose focus and the person will become stupefied. Therefore, one must train the mind to focus on one point first. That is the key to pacifying the mind.

There are five families in Esoteric Buddhism, and the first is the tathagata family, also known as the buddha family. The principal buddha of the buddha family is Vairocana Buddha. The mother of the tathagata family is Buddha-Eye Bodhisattva (Locana). Vairocana is flanked by Golden-Wheel Vajra, wrathful Acala and Acala's consort Aparajita-Vidyarajni. The heart of the tathagata family conceals the secret mantra, and the mandala is surrounded by many attendants. These constitute the divisions of the buddha family. When we begin the practice of Mahamudra, we must first learn the meditation posture of Vairocana, so that we may gain access into the buddha family and attain buddhahood in this very body.

Meditating in the full-lotus position allows the winds [qi] to flow and circulate in the lower body. Therefore, it is not just an aesthetic pose. This position facilitates the smooth circulation of the downward-moving wind.

Place the hands evenly [on your lap], with the tips of the middle fingers touching each other, and keep the thumbs close to the lower portion of the index fingers. This helps the body and mind to stay completely composed, and also improves the balance of the body temperature, the circulation of winds, and the blood circulation.

By raising the chest and tucking the chin in, the winds can circulate smoothly throughout the whole body. If we do not maintain a good posture, there will not be a sufficient amount of winds available and we will likely doze off during practice. Many people have asked me why they fall asleep during meditation. This is the result of not raising the chest or tucking the chin, which leads to absence of winds. Too much relaxation will lead one to fall asleep.

When the tongue is pressed against the upper palate, it allows the upward-moving wind to move downwards, and the downward-moving wind to move upwards. The two winds mutually nourish each other through this approach. This important point shall be elucidated on in Chapter Four.

The act of gazing at an object is also the same method of Focusing on the Tianxin Spot [located at the forehead; also known as the seat of the spiritual eye] introduced in the book, *The Illuminated Way of Meditation*. By focusing the mind, one enters into meditative absorption. We can hold a vajra about five and a half feet away from us and gaze at it. When we look at the vajra, we should revere it as though it were the Chinese emperor's long jade tablet. This will make the meditation more meaningful and tangible.

Vairocana, the Great Sun Tathagata, once expounded dharma at Mahesvara's palace. At that time, the golden-colored, glittering Vairocana wore a hairknot crown with the Five Buddhas sitting above. He radiated many colored lights and was dressed in a white silk celestial robe. His majestic manifestation serves as evidence of his perfect enlightenment in the Suddhavasa Heaven. Some people assume that

Vairocana, the Great Sun Tathagata, is the Sun God. Although the Great Sun Tathagata is synonymous with the sun itself, which turns darkness into brightness, I feel that sunlight is also divided into day and night, and there are places where sunlight can never reach. Thus, the word "great" is added to the word "sun" to signify that the light of the Buddha is prevalent in the day, night, and inside or outside, because the wisdom light of the Great Sun Tathagata shines throughout all dharma realms with equal strength.

I shall tell a secret to my readers. When Vairocana was teaching in the Palace of Mahesvara, there was a kumara [child] in the audience whose name was Padmakumara.

Padmakumara placed his palms together in respect and asked the Buddha, "Why is the Tathagata seen sitting, and not standing?"

"To sit is to abide in the great dharma realm of tranquility. I make full use of the seven- point meditation posture to instruct sentient beings."

"How should they be instructed?" Padmakumara asked.

"By means of Mahamudra, which is constant and indestructible, and harmonizes the body and mind."

Padmakumara's questions initiated a series of events where I would deliver sentient beings at a specific time in the distant future as Padmakumara. I accepted the decree of Vairocana and manifested here as Padmakumara to transmit the Mahamudra. This is how it all started. The event was a celestial secret, which was neither mysterious nor improvised. Everything has its cause and effect.

Mahamudra is anything but simple. One begins with the seven-point posture of Vairocana, which balances and controls the functions of the winds and channels. Through the techniques of the full-lotus position, meditation mudra, raising the chest, tucking the chin, pressing the tongue against the upper palate, and gazing at an object, the body and mind are harmonized. Only by mastering these prerequisites and setting a good practice foundation can one begin to cultivate the essential teachings of purity and perfect realization. Before one can arrive at the state of non-meditation and non-attainment, one should start with the preliminaries and attain fruition in meditation.

Mahamudra involves the practice of winds, channels, and light drops. This is the approach for attaining buddhahood in this very body. It is not an empty theory. It requires the individual to put it into vigorous practice, to cultivate, and to gain a real spiritual response. After that the cultivator shall know that I, Sheng-yen Lu, did not make this up and what I have said here is absolutely true.

Through fearless expedient means, I lead individuals through my teachings so that they may be liberated from the suffering of this world, and generate the causes and conditions of buddhahood to attain the path of liberation.

Sheng-yen Lu

4. Psychic Heat, Drops and Inner Fire

The city of Seattle is situated in the State of Washington in the United States. Washington is in the northwest region of America, and shares a border with Canada. This state is five times the size of Taiwan, and has a population of four million [as of 1984]. Because it is located in the north, it is freezing cold in the winter. In the winter of 1983, a heavy snow reduced the temperature to minus thirty degrees Celsius at night, with a daytime temperature of around minus ten degrees.

At that time, the rivers and lakes were frozen. I carried a pail of water outside and it turned into a big ice cube in an instant. Everything was covered with snow and ice. Many household pipes or car radiators burst or cracked. Accidents of different kinds were visible all around, due to the difficulties of controlling the cars on ice.

Even pen ink was frozen, not to mention the dew on the windows of my True Buddha Attic that had also turned into ice. Nonetheless, I continued with my meditation, without a heater in the attic. In the severe cold winter, I had to rely on the heat generated through Maha-mudra to counter the freezing cold. In my attic the cold air had consolidated into ice, yet my body was sweating lightly like a stove that was warm all over. This is the psychic heat or inner heat produced by Mahamudra practice.

Here is the method for producing psychic heat:

We stabilize ourselves with the seven-point posture of Vairocana and regulate our breathing.

Visualize a spot about four fingers beneath the navel. It is a place where the three channels, the left channel, the right channel and the middle channel converge, which is known to the Taoists as the dan-tian. In this spot there is the Sanskrit syllable half AH which has the width of a hair follicle and appears red. This half AH trembles and vibrates like the flame that trembles in a stove. In your visualization, feel that the little flame residing at the junction of the three channels is warm.

While one is still seated, breathe in using the complete inhalation approach, so that the wind enters the left and right channels (One may review this breathing method in my book, *The Realization of the Master*). When this breath of wind reaches the meeting point of the three channels, it fans the fire and increases the temperature of the red fiery flame. Consequently the short AH, that is as thin as a strand of hair, thickens and becomes even redder.

While performing complete breathing, one needs to visualize the exhalation of blue smoke. Thus each complete inhalation and exhalation is synchronized with the respective visualizations, and one continues this cycle of breathing.

Each inhalation and exhalation performed is called a breathing cycle. By performing ten such breathing cycles, the flame should reach the solar plexus chakra [located one to two inches above the navel]. With the next ten breathing cycles, the solar plexus chakra and its surrounding area should be filled with heated winds. The subsequent ten breathing cycles should cause the lower body to experience warmth all over. Another ten breathing cycles thereafter should raise the flame to the heart chakra. Another ten breathing cycles should move it further upwards to the throat chakra. Then, the next ten breathing cycles should raise the flame towards the third-eye chakra. Another ten breathing cycles should lead it to the crown chakra.

Once I heard that there was a highly adept monk who would place a teapot of cold water upon his head every time he sat in meditation. When the monk entered into meditative absorption, his body would remain very still. An hour later, the cold water in the teapot would turn hot and begin steaming. Such a feat is the yoga of psychic heat, which is the practice of drops and inner fire.

Those who are less adept in this practice may achieve a warm sensation around the region of the dantian. Even one's lower body region feels like a stove and feels hot when touched with the hand.

When one gains mastery over the yoga of psychic heat, even the most subtle spots such as the cold tips of the fingers and toes can be penetrated by the heat of the winds. The whole body experiences a hot sensation. This is the reason why I could keep myself warm during the freezing cold winter.

When the psychic heat reaches the crown chakra, the white bodhicitta (white drops) at the crown chakra melts and drips downwards via the path of the tongue that is pressing against the upper palate. This fluid is known in Taoism as the heavenly court water, and is called nectar in Buddhism. The fluid has the characteristic of being cool and when it is mixed with the psychic heat, it produces a nurturing effect. This is known as the "mixing of water and fire."

On the practice of psychic heat and the practice of inner fire and drops, I would like to elucidate the main points one more time:

1. The first experience that marks progress on the path to attainment of buddhahood through Mahamudra is psychic heat. When the psychic heat is ignited, it signals success in the most elementary achievement. Without it, it is all

empty talk. Some practitioners have gone astray with their practices. As a result, they have lost their glow and their limbs have become cold. These symptoms are an indication of a practice gone wrong.

2. The initial practice of the Mahamudra of psychic heat requires one to meditate six times daily, and only after the ignition of psychic heat can one reduce the practice to three or four times a day. Each session requires at least seventy breathing cycles. One round of inhaling and exhaling constitutes one breathing cycle.

3. The syllable AH is Sanskrit, and the half AH that is as thin as a hair breath resembles the Chinese character Na with the right portion removed. During visualization, pay special attention to the blazing red syllable becoming more red and thicker, and as the flame grows, it gets hotter as the practice progresses.

4. Inhale through the complete breathing method. Keep the breath slow and drawn out, so that it reaches the meeting point at the dantian. With the winds fanning the fire, the fire blazes upwards fiercely, moving through one chakra every ten breathing cycles. In total, seventy breaths are needed every meditation session for the seven chakras. Some practice one hundred and eight breathing cycles, penetrating all the meridians in the body.

5. When the psychic heat blazes up to the crown chakra, the white bodhicitta (nectar) melts and drips downwards. This is a method of mixing water and fire. This is a great secret within heaven and earth, and a major celestial secret indeed. The truth of attainment in Buddhism is found within this practice, and it also contains the truth of the formation of relics (sariras).

6. One must exhale through complete breathing as well.

Keep the breath slow and drawn out and visualize blue smoke leaving one's body, which is similar to how smoke from a stove leaves the chimney.

7. There is a sensation associated with the cultivation of psychic heat. The coldness of the limbs is removed, and those with health problems find relief when the fire of the psychic heat burns inwardly. The circulation of the inner fire of psychic heat clears the meridians of blockages, and those who gain mastery over its application may find themselves immune to illnesses. This is certainly a vital method for balancing the spiritual energies of body and mind.

8. Due to the arousal of psychic heat, the body feels warm all over and the individual finds himself bathed in the feeling of lightness. The body feels very light where the mind enjoys a state of freedom. Discursive thoughts cease, leaving the person in a condition of extreme tranquility and joy. Generally speaking, as one moves further into the practice, many stages of phenomena may be experienced, such as visions of past lives, and images of beautiful women and dream-like illusory imageries. Irrespective of the nature of these illusory visions, whether they are good or bad, we should not attach to them. Instead, we should aim for active and diligent cultivation that will naturally lead us to achieve samadhi.

Someone once asked me what psychic heat and inner fire were. The true meaning of psychic heat is the breath of life [prana]. The true meaning of inner fire is the fire of life. The survival of man hinges on psychic heat and inner fire.

What exactly is the central channel? The central channel is an invisible channel, a pathway that facilitates the travel of psychic heat through the body. In principle, it exists and moves through the center of the spine, and some of its secondary veins fan out from the spine. Some have said that the central channel is the governing center of all spiritual veins. It is close to the mingmen meridian, the gate of life, which is the source of life itself. The Indians called it the muladhara, the seat of all drops of psychic heat. These drops are the very life drops of humans, and the body is born from these drops.

Today, the teachings of Mahamudra have clearly elucidated the basic source of life for humankind, and it explains in detail the way to produce psychic heat and inner fire. My exposition on all these teachings is geared towards delivering all sentient beings. Through fearless expedient means, I lead individuals through my teachings so that they may be liberated from the suffering of this world, and generate the causes and conditions of buddhahood to attain the path of liberation. What a great dharma affinity and secret this is! The practice of psychic heat requires perseverance, moving from the simple to deep levels, and from the deep levels one enters into the wonderful realms. From the wonderful realms one enters into the mystical realm, through which realization can be attained.

Many are aware that I am afraid of hot weather but not cold weather. This is due to the fact that I have long achieved the cultivation of psychic heat and the cultivation of drops and inner fire.

Many are also aware that Sheng-yen Lu has great supernatural power, while others have called me a con man with no ability of any sort! Yet the fact that I can write about the practice of Mahamudra is an evidence of a true and thorough understanding. There is nothing mystical about this, for it is the fruit of my actual practice. I have walked past this secret gate and have truly mastered its secrets.

5. Genuine Practice of Speech Purification

I would like to first draw your attention to a little story and after-wards, we can learn more about the genuine practice of speech purification:

A certain celestial being, whose name was Immortal Benevolent Fruit, resided in the Heaven of Constant Enjoyment in the Realm of Desire. Because his heaven was adjacent to the human world, he often received offerings from humans and frequently contacted me. Though he had enjoyed great meritorious blessings in the celestial realm, he had not continued any form of cultivation. When his blessings came to an end, he displayed the five decaying signs of a celestial being.

The five decaying signs of a celestial being are:

1. The clean celestial clothing suddenly becomes tainted.
2. The adornments of crown and flowers on the head suddenly lose their shine and start to wither.
3. The aura of light emitted from the godly being suddenly [becomes dim], and the body emits a stench and releases odor.

4. Sweat is seen at the armpit. Before, the being could travel to any realm at will but afterwards, he is bound to one place and loses all his transformative power.
5. The godly being begins to feel agitated and dislikes his present condition.

When Immortal Benevolent Fruit experienced the celestial beings' five signs of decay, I was the only one he could turn to for help. As an inhabitant in the Heaven of Constant Enjoyment, where the celestial citizens enjoy the fruits of their blessings, he had been living with the attitude of "enjoy the blessings now and worry about the future later." The beings that reside in this heaven absolutely do not care about cultivation. Thus their state is less ideal, [in terms of dharma diligence], than beings in the physical world. Life in samsara includes both suffering and joy, so it motivates people to cultivate because they aspire to be liberated from suffering.

If a human performs meritorious deeds, he ascends to the Heaven of Constant Enjoyment to rejoice in his blessings. Because he does not know how to cultivate the right dharma; however, he is subject to the phenomenon of the celestial beings' five signs of decay when his blessings have been used up. (These facts are detailed in the sutras.)

Immortal Benevolent Fruit came to me and said, "Lian-sheng, you must help me."

"You are experiencing the five signs of decay?" I asked.

"Yes."

"You're my friend. I will definitely help you."

In my meditation, I formed the Mudra of the Bodhi Middle Way and transformed the spirit of Immortal Benevolent Fruit into a sleeping baby. Then I sealed up the original nature of the immortal being, so that his mind would not wander, and he remained in a constant state of meditative contemplation. I taught Immortal Benevolent Fruit to abide in the self-nature of his mind and recite the mantra *Om ah hum guru-bei ah-ha-sa-sa-ma-ha lian-sheng siddhi hum,* focusing only on the recitation of this mantra and ignoring everything else.

When one cannot speak, it is called the purification of speech. When the body cannot move, it is called the purification of body. The mind itself is mantra, and mantra is the "true word" that continues without cessation. This is called purifying the mind, where one stays in a perpetual state of meditative contemplation.

By using the Bodhi Middle Way Mudra, I sent Immortal Benevolent Fruit to the world of changing phenomena, where he incarnated to the human realm. As a baby, he was born mute. In this respect, he abided by speech purification. The baby was born with the condition of having soft bones, where he could not move or stand. In this way, he abided by body purification.

The baby was handicapped at birth, born with the condition of soft bones, and was speech impaired. He found two people who were karmically indebted to him, and required them to care for him, worry about his needs, protect him, treat his ailments, and so forth.

Yet, no one was aware that the baby was the reincarnation of Immortal Benevolent Fruit. The only thing that he knew was that his self-nature resided in his heart and he never ceased reciting the mantra: *Om ah hum guru-bei ah-ha-sa-sa-ma-ha lian-sheng siddhi hum.* Immortal Benevolent Fruit was unperturbed by anything, and concentrated only on his mantra recitation within the confinement of his little physical body.

As he was unable to speak, there was no opportunity for him to create speech karma. Because he was unable to move, there was no opportunity for him to create body karma. And since his mind was reciting the mantra, he was engaged in genuine cultivation.

Therefore, Immortal Benevolent Fruit was unafraid of being tainted by the human world. Otherwise, he might never be free from its bondage. Hence he was overwhelmed with joy and upon the death of the baby, his spirit ascended to the Maha Twin Lotus Ponds at the

Western Paradise of Ultimate Bliss. This was due to the result of his genuine cultivation. Immortal Benevolent Fruit later achieved great accomplishments. My use of the Bodhi Middle Way Mudra had helped him. This is a true story.

I began the chapter with this story, and leave it out there for anyone to believe or disbelieve. It is really up to you.

So what exactly is the true practice of speech purification? In principle, those who practice the Mahamudra are considered to be true renunciates. This is the meaning of true retreat, which is not concerned with retreat in the mountains, in caves or stone houses, but it refers to a retreat that occurs within the thoughts and speech of one's body. This is the retreat of the mind and not the body, which makes it an invisible retreat. When we close off the speech and mind of the physical body, which is made up of the four elements, we attain the true state of retreat. Genuine retreat is essentially the enclosure of the six root senses.

The actual state of Mahamudra is a state of True Voidness, known as Sunyata in Sanskrit. It does not refer to a world of total emptiness where absolutely nothing exists. It is the state of true reality. As we abide in a state of cultivation, we are not subjected to the arising of the senses, maintaining an attitude of neither yes nor no, good nor bad. We maintain this meditative insight, remaining silent in our speech and keeping the body in a calm and tranquil state. This cultivation approach is similar to the way Immortal Benevolent Fruit had maintained his mind.

The state of a baby's sweet slumber reflects the true purified state of one practicing Mahamudra, for at that time no discursive thoughts exist in the mind, which itself is free from any other thought forms. The body also remains calm and still. When one practices in this fashion, it won't take long before one gains realization. In other words, this situation in which the heart remains undistracted is a state of complete purity, which includes the purification of speech, body and mind. These states of purification of body, speech and mind are interconnected and undivided. Those who cultivate with these three purification secret tantras shall attain yogic response. Their practice of Mahamudra will achieve fruition.

When we ignite the psychic heat, which passes through the crown chakra, we may visualize the guru appearing as Padmakumara above the crown chakra, wearing the five-buddha crown and dressed in his dharma robe. His right hand holds a vajra and his left hand holds a bell. Two strips of cloth printed with the Six Syllable Mantra *Om, mani padme, hum* hang from his crown to his shoulders. Padmakumara is seated on an eight-petalled lotus throne and its stem reaches down beneath the throne through the crown chakra of the practitioner. Then the practitioner circulates his psychic heat through the stem of the eight-petalled lotus. As the practitioner's psychic heat arises, reaching and becoming one with the Guru, the psychic heat from the Guru also descends into the practitioner. This two-way energy exchange results in a condition called "Bliss through the Arising of Wisdom." This constitutes the great yogic response of Guru Yoga.

When one enters into such a deep, profound state of meditation, everything relies on the maneuvering of the mind. The exhalation of breath is slow and drawn out, and similarly, the inhalation is equally slow and drawn out. The exhaling and inhaling of the breath is delicate and subtle. The heartbeat is calm, and all digestive functions, excretion, blood circulation and sensation are reduced to a minimum. This is the phenomenon of the three purifications that are experienced when the six root senses are shut off, which resembles the condition of a baby in sweet slumber.

During this period of cultivation, all three delusions are eliminated: delusions arising from incorrect views and thoughts, delusions arising from detailed observation, and delusions arising from ignorance. Following the elimination of delusions, three wisdoms arise: the wisdom of omniscience, the wisdom of adaptive means, and the wisdom of all-inclusive cognition. This leads to the attainment of the wisdom eye, the dharma eye and the buddha eye, and attainment of three virtues: the virtue of prajna, the virtue of liberation, and the virtue of the dharmakaya. Mahamudra is therefore the highest form of wisdom.

By reviewing the incident of Immortal Benevolent Fruit and using the example of a baby's sweet slumber as a metaphor to point to the actual state of attainment, one can better understand the genuine practice of speech purification. When one practices in such a [confined] stage, one actualizes the Bodhi Middle Path, in which the body, speech and mind are inter-related and mutually complemented. The purification of body, speech, and mind are inseparable. One is three and three is one. This is the essence of the body, speech, and mind perfectly complementing each other.

6. Fourfold Mindfulness of Nagarjuna

The name Nagarjuna was translated into Chinese in three different renderings, namely Longshu [Dragon Tree], Longsheng [Dragon Victory] and Longmeng [Dragon Vigor].The term "Longtian" [Dragon Sky] in Chinese that is often mentioned actually refers to the two Bodhisattvas, Longshu [Nagarjuna] and Tianqin [Vasubandhu].

Nagarjuna ranks third in the transmission lineage of the Eight Shingon Patriarchs, and ranks first among the Eight Shingon Lineage Torchbearers. Nagarjuna was the disciple of the Thirteenth Zen Patriarch, Kapimala. Nagabodhi founded Vajrayana after Nagarjuna's time, but since Nagarjuna had already received the Surangama Samadhi, the official establishment of Vajrayana named Nagarjuna as its founder.

The Sanskrit name for Longshu Bodhisattva is Nagarjuna. The image of Nagarjuna is carved as the form of a solitary hearer dressed in a monk's robe, seated on the lotus throne with his palms placed together. This image resembles an arhat. There is mystery and legend surrounding every aspect of Nagarjuna's life. As an exceptional person with holy characteristics, he could commit any sutras to memory at a glance. He enjoyed a widespread reputation. Before he was ordained as a monk, he was especially fond of women, indulging himself in lustful pursuits. It was only later, when he realized the uselessness of sexual indulgence, that he decided to leave the material world in search of the Buddhist path of renunciation. In a period of ninety days, he read the entire Tripitaka [the three Buddhist canons] and completely understood all the profound doctrines.

The great Bodhisattva Nagarjuna should be credited for the flourishing of Mahayana Buddhism. He was born into a Brahmin family sometime in the last quarter of the second century CE, in Vidarbha in southern India. He passed away in the last quarter of the third century.

A famous account of Nagarjuna depicts him receiving the transmission of the Mahayana sutras from an old monk while he was practicing in the Himalayas. After that, he became engrossed in the works of Mahayana. Because his ancestral link could be traced to the nagas or dragons of northern India, Nagarjuna was able to enter the dragon palace beneath the ocean by using his spiritual powers. Inside, he studied all the Mahayana sutras that were housed there, made his own records and brought the scriptures back. This was the reason why Mahayana Buddhism prospered.

When Nagarjuna was spreading the Dharma in southern India, he defeated many heretics. When he expounded the Mahayana teachings in the monastery of Black Bee Mountain, many Hinayana monks and others from the Black Sect were persuaded and impressed by his superior wisdom. According to the events recorded in the biography of Nagarjuna, he wrote *Hundred Thousand Verses of Upadesa, Five Thousand Verses on the Treatise of Adorning the Buddhahood, Fifty Verses on the Treatise of the Expedient Means of Great Compassion*, and *Hundred Thousand Verses of the Treatise of Fearlessness*, from which the *Madhyamaka-sastra* was derived. His works were numerous. Thus, he was revered as the Lord of a Thousand Treatises.

To my knowledge, Nagarjuna was one of the manifestations of Amitabha Buddha. Therefore, among the Five Buddhas, he is Amitabha. We can find many of his works in Buddhist libraries including the following:

Treatise on the Materials for Bodhi
Friendly Epistles [Surl-lekha]
Compilation of Sutras of the Canopy of Blessings and Right Actions [Sutrasamuccaya]
Treatise on the Twelve Gates [Dvadasa-dvara Sastra]
Fundamentals of the Middle Way [MulamadhyamakaKarikas]
Treatise on the Eighteen Kinds of Sunyata [Astadasakasa Sastra]
Refutation of the Concept of Being in the Mahayana [Bhavasamkranti]
Treatise on the Essence of Expediency, Commentary on the Great Prajnaparamita Sastra [Mahaprajnaparamita Sastra]
Exposition of the Ten Stages of Bodhisattvahood [Dasabhumivibhasa Sastra]
Verses in Praise of the Dharma Realm
Treatise of the Absence of Bodhicitta
Verses on the Greatness of Making of Vows
Averting Arguments [Vigraha-vyavartani]
Treatise of Many Minds
Treatise of the Thirty-Seven Stanzas
Four Treatises on Right Mindfulness
Treatise on the Auspicious Blessings

There are also others.

Compared to others, Nagarjuna's knowledge was most profound and wide-ranging, so he was able to bring Mahayana Buddhism into blossom. He was able to fulfill his bodhisattva mission of propagating the seeds of Buddha-dharma on a large scale.

The history of Nagarjuna's life is infused with many legends. Some

Tibetan lamas said that Nagarjuna was born during the first century BCE. Other lamas said that he was born four hundred years after Sakyamuni Buddha entered into pari-nirvana. There was also a saying that Nagarjuna lived for six hundred years. Other sources mentioned that he was still expounding the dharma between the second and third centuries CE.

So, why do I mention Nagarjuna in my writing about Mahamudra? It is because Nagarjuna is the first lineage holder of Vajrayana. He spoke the Dharma to the king of southern India who was committed to the Buddha-dharma, and made Nagarjuna his imperial advisor. Nagarjuna elucidated the doctrines of the Middle Path as found in the *Commentary on the Great Prajnaparamita Sastra*. These doctrines, he explained, are the Fourfold Mindfulness of Mahamudra.

The Fourfold Mindfulness as taught by Nagarjuna is as follows:

1. Mindfulness of the body - Contemplation on the empty nature of the body.
2. Mindfulness of the suffering caused by emotions - Contemplation on the five aggregates, which are empty in nature.
3. Mindfulness of the mind - Contemplation on the non-origination and non-extinction of all phenomena.
4. Mindfulness of phenomena - Ceaseless contemplation on the first three kinds of mindfulness.

I shall elucidate on this further:

Mindfulness of the body - As Buddhists that practice Mahamudra, it is necessary to remind ourselves to frequently practice mindfulness of the body, visualizing our fathers on our right and our mothers on our left, along with all of our parents, relatives and loved ones in the six realms surrounding us. The hell realm is located the closest to us. Lying further away is the hungry ghost realm. After that is the animal realm, followed by the human realm. Further away is the asura realm, and the furthest is the heavenly realm.

If one does not cultivate the Buddha-dharma, eventually he will become spiritually degenerated. This is true for all sentient beings. All of us who are mindful of ourselves in the physical body know that physical phenomena must undergo the four stages of completion, existence, destruction and finally emptiness. Likewise, everyone is subject to birth, old age, sickness and death. Thus, when observing the mindfulness of the body, it is important to contemplate on the empty nature of the body. As stated in the *Diamond Sutra*, we must see through the delusion of the physical and egotistical self. The perception of a self, a being, a life, and a soul is essentially empty.

Being mindful of the body means to contemplate on its empty nature. One who is deluded is an ordinary mortal. One who is enlightened is a buddha.

This concept of mindfulness of the body is fundamentally similar to concepts that one first learns in studying Buddhism, and may appear to be "elementary." Nonetheless, not many people are able to see through the delusion of the body. Many are aware that "all material things will eventually be destroyed, and all living things will age and die," and that no one is excluded from this natural process. However, those who cannot see through the delusion of the body will continue to pursue fame, fortune and other material things. These deluded people will naturally fall into the three lower realms and will be drawn back into the six realms of samsara.

Thus, constant contemplation on mindfulness of the body involves contemplation on the empty nature of the physical body, and it is the first step in seeking renunciation.

Mindfulness of the suffering caused by emotions - The five aggregates are born from five kinds of discursive thoughts, and are certainly not a part of the nature of True Reality or Suchness. The cause and effect of these two are linked and mutually dependent. The five aggregates are the aggregates of form, feeling, conception, habitual action and consciousness. The aggregate of form refers to physical form. The aggregate of sensation is the feeling caused by the perception of physical objects. The aggregate of conception is the arising of thoughts. The aggregate of habitual action refers to unfocused mental formations and unrefined actions. The aggregate of consciousness is the mental faculty that is responsible for all changes and transformations.

In principle, the arising of the five aggregates stems from a defiled thought, which results in the confusion between true reality and delusion. In turn, this forms the aggregate of consciousness. From consciousness arise the aggregates of form, sensation, conception and habitual action. They overlap one another and arise in stages.

Generally speaking, it is necessary to first eliminate the aggregate of form before attempting to eliminate all five aggregates. The root of all aggregates stems from the rise of discursive thoughts. Sakyamuni Buddha once said, "The five aggregates are rooted in delusions, and yet the inherit nature of our true mind is pristine and sublime. It is inherently pure and perfect, and is devoid of thoughts and contamination. Even though the true essence of our self-awareness was originally wonderful and clean, when a single thought drifts due to karmic affinity, the five aggregates arise, and the drifting thought subsequently transforms into delusion."

For this reason, the Buddhist practitioner of Mahamudra must recognize the delusion and emptiness of the five aggregates by being mindful of the suffering caused by emotion. Once he sees through this, he will naturally develop disdain for the cycle of life and death. Ultimately, he will understand the mindfulness of emotion afflictions, contemplate on the five aggregates, long for the genuine bliss of nirvana, and no longer foolishly attach to the burning house of the three lower realms.

Mindfulness of the mind - Contemplation on the non-origination and non-extinction of all mental phenomena. Here is a verse: "The nature of phenomena arising from mental conditions is marked by non-origination, non-extinction, non-destruction, non-permanence, non-coming into being, non-going out of being, non-identity, and non-differentiation. With the cessation of all deluded concepts, I pay homage to the buddhas who have expounded the wonderful teachings of tranquility."

The Buddhist practitioner of Mahamudra should contemplate on the world as being created from the thoughts of sentient beings. This is like the saying, "the three realms are created by the mind, and all phenomena are formed from consciousness." We must first pacify the discursive mind. Then the six defilements [generated from the tainted six faculties will cease to arise, and the karmic obscurations will be eliminated too. When one arrives at the stage where no thought arises, the six realms of cyclic existence will disappear and one will be liberated from the three lower realms.

The statement "the three realms are created by the mind, and all phenomena are formed from consciousness" illustrates the reality that all phenomena are marked by non-origination and non-extinction. By understanding that "all phenomena are marked by non-origination and non-extinction," one realizes that "emptiness and illusion are non-dual and undifferentiated. [At the level of realization,] there is no love or hatred, no giving or taking, and no mind of grasping or craving. The mind of equanimity is well engendered and fortified. One will then bring awakening and liberation to oneself and others. That is the perfect realization and complete practice of the bodhisattva's mindfulness of the mind.

Mindfulness of mental phenomena - The Mahamudra practitioner must constantly and vigilantly contemplate on the first three states of mindfulness. One should not take the concepts lightly and practice it with a negligent attitude. Nagarjuna's method of contemplating on the four forms of mindfulness leads to the silencing of all discursive thoughts, thereby help one to gain the great perfection of Mahamudra.

Here's a verse:

> One must contemplate on the nature of the dharma realm,
> The body, sensations and mind are mental states.
> Mahamudra itself is a Dharma.
> It expresses the doctrine of the Middle Way.

7. Blessings of the Guru on Mahamudra

Anyone who practices Mahamudra must pray to his guru for blessings prior to entering each meditation session. The following is how Tibetan lamas recite the Lineage Prayers of Invocation [Dorje Chang Thungma]:

DOR JÉ CHANG CHEN TÉLO NARO DANG
Great Vajradhara, Tilopa, Naropa,

MARPA MILA CHÖ-JE GAMPOPA
Marpa, Milarepa, and Lord of the Dharma, Gampopa,

DÜSUM SHÉ JA KÜN KHYEN KARMAPA
Knower of the three times, omniscient Karmapa,

CHÉ ZHI CHUNG GYE GYÜ PA DZIN NAM DANG
Lineage holders of the four major and eight minor schools:

DRI TAK TSAL SUM PALDEN DRUKPA SOK
Drikung, Taklung, Tsalpa, glorious Drukpa and others;

ZAB LAM CHAK GYA CHÉ LA NGA NYÉ PÉ
You who have thoroughly mastered the profound path of Mahamudra,

NYAM MÉ DRO GÖN DAKPO KAGYÜ-LA
Unrivaled protectors of beings, the Dakpo Kagyü,

SOLWA DEB SO KAGYÜ LAMA NAM
I pray to you, the Kagyü lamas,

GYÜ PA DZIN NO NAM TAR JIN GYI LOB
Grant your blessings that we may follow your tradition and example.

ZHEN LOK GOM GYI KANG PAR SUNG PA ZHIN
It is taught that detachment is the foot of meditation.

ZÉ NOR KÜN LA CHAK ZHEN MÉ PA DANG
Attachment to food and wealth disappears,

TSEN DIR DÖ TAK CHÖ PAY GOM CHEN LA
To the meditator who gives up his ties to this life;

NYE KUR ZHEN PA ME PAR JIN GYI LOB
Grant your blessings so that attachment to ownership and honor will cease.

MÖ GÖ GOM GYI GO WOR SUNG PA ZHIN
It is taught that devotion is the head of meditation,

MEN NGAK TER GO JÉ PAY LAMA LA
The lama opens the door to the profound oral teachings;

GYÜN DU SOLWA DEB PAY GOM CHEN LA
To the meditator who always turns to him,

CHÖ MIN MÖ GÜ KYÉ WAR JIN GYI LOB
Grant your blessing that uncontrived devotion be born from within.

YENG MÉ GOM GYI NGÖ ZHIR SUNG PA ZHIN
It is taught that unwavering attention is the body of meditation.

GANG SHAR TOK PAY NGO WO SO MA DÉ
Whatever arises is the fresh nature of thought;

MA CHÖ DÉ KAR JOK PAY GOM CHEN LA
To the meditator who rests in naturalness,

GOM JA LO DANG DRAL WAR JIN GYI LOB
Grant your blessings that meditation be free from intellectualization.

NAM TOK NGO WO CHÖ KUR SUNG PA ZHIN
The essence of thought is dharmakaya, it is taught.

CHI YANG MA YIN CHIR YANG CHAR WA LA
Thoughts are nothing whatsoever, and yet they arise in the mind;

MA GAK ROL PAR CHHAR WAY GOM CHHEN LA
To the meditator who reflects upon the unobstructed play of the mind,

KHOR DÉ JER MÉ TOK PAR JIN GYI LOB
Grant your blessing that the inseparability of samsara and nirvana be realized.

KYÉ WA KÜN TU YANG DAK LAMA DANG
Through all my births, may I not be separated

DRAL MÉ CHÖ KYI PAL LA LONG CHÖ CHING
From the perfect Lama and so enjoy the glory of the Dharma.

SA DANG LA GYI YÖN TEN RAP DZOK NÉ
May I completely accomplish the qualities of the path and all stages,

DOR JÉ CHANG GI GO P'HANG NYUR TOP SHOK
And quickly attain the state of Vajradhara.

Those who recite this prayer in Tibetan should take note of these points:

1. This prayer is a Chinese transliteration from the Tibetan language, and is provided only as a reference. As the local dialect differs from province to province, correct pronunciation of the prayer may not be achieved. If one aspires to recite it properly, then it is best to seek guidance from a Tibetan lama. However, each lama may pronounce the prayer differently, as the Tibetan language is colored by many different local accents.
2. This phonetic transcription, taught to me by a disciple of the Sixteenth Karmapa, already approximates to the Tibetan sounds.
3. Words such as DANG, PA, SOK, PÉ, LA, ZHIN, DÉ and

LOB signify the end of a sentence.

4. ER is an ending sound that can be pronounced half-tone, with the latter pitch dropped.

When one aspires to practice the Mahamudra, one must receive the necessary empowerments and oral teachings from the root guru. The practitioner must first establish yogic union with the living guru, and through him seek union with the lineage holders . Only by achieving union in this lineage sequence can one gain accomplishments. This is because the Mahamudra practitioner needs to rely on the blessings of the guru, and rely on the guru's holy mind to cleanse one's defiled mind. When the practitioner gains a secret union in which one's mind is in tune with the guru's mind, one shall have great accomplishment.

The guru is the embodiment of the Triple Jewels of the Buddha, Dharma and Sangha. When one takes refuge in the guru, it is tantamount to taking refuge in the Dharmakaya Buddha. Such great accomplishment must begin with taking refuge, where a person cleanses oneself of karma by transforming karma into right wisdom. This constitutes the first step of a mundane being stepping into buddhahood.

The grace of the guru bestowed upon the practitioner will open the spirit and mind, for the guru's spiritual light is omnipresent and resides in space. The guru is one who has realized the nirvana of perfect enlightenment through his practice of the Highest Yoga of Mahamudra. Such is the great spiritual mother light that spans all space. Through empowerment, the human guru and lineage holders are transformed into globes of spiritual light that enter the practitioner through his crown chakra. Only then can one gain Mahamudra fruition.

The guru's blessing in Mahamudra is performed by visualizing one's human guru on one's crown chakra. Above the guru, there are seated the lineage holders in yoga posture in multiple levels, arranged in ascending order, beginning with the human guru at the base and Vajradhara [Dorje Chang in Tibetan at the top]. In this case, the guru is Holy Red Crown Vajra Guru Master Lian-sheng, Sheng-yen Lu. Above him, the Sixteenth Gyalwa Karmapa and so forth are seated. Visualize the lineage holders transforming into light drops that are absorbed into one's body, uniting with the gurus, and emitting the great spiritual light.

Here are the verses of praise for the blessings of Mahamudra:

> To all gurus: I pray to you,
> Bestow your great spiritual light upon me.
> Grant that all is complete and continues without pause
> In my practice of Mahamudra.

> To all gurus: I pray to you,
> Bestow your great spiritual light upon me.
> Grant that I shall become the mandala itself
> In my practice of Mahamudra.

> To all gurus: I pray to you,
> Bestow your great spiritual light upon me.
> Grant that my three channels will be filled
> In my practice of Mahamudra.

> To all gurus: I pray to you
> Bestow your great spiritual light upon me.
> Grant that my body shall be filled with psychic heat
> In my practice of Mahamudra.

> To all gurus: I pray to you,
> Bestow your great spiritual light upon me.
> Grant that all impurities shall be purified
> In my practice of Mahamudra.

To all gurus: I pray to you,
Bestow your great spiritual light upon me.
Grant that the dharmakaya shall soon appear
In my practice of Mahamudra.

To all gurus: I pray to you,
Bestow your great spiritual light upon me.
Grant that I shall be freed from delusion
In my practice of Mahamudra.
To all gurus: I pray to you,
Bestow your great spiritual light upon me.
Grant that I shall attain buddhahood soon
In my practice of Mahamudra.

To all gurus: I pray to you,
Bestow your great spiritual light upon me.
Grant that my consciousness will be transformed
In my practice of Mahamudra, so that I may turn the dharma
wheel.

To all gurus: I pray to you,
Bestow your great spiritual light upon me.
Grant that I shall attain great accomplishment
In my practice of Mahamudra.

To all gurus: I pray to you,
Bestow your great spiritual light upon me.
Grant that I shall swiftly attain nirvana
In my practice of Mahamudra

Before every meditation session, we must first recite the Supplication for the Blessing of Living Buddha Lian-sheng [from the *True*

Buddha Sutra], and then visualize the human guru and all lineage holders transforming into light drops that enter our body. Afterwards, we need to recite the verses for the blessing of Mahamudra. Next, we may begin to practice. The various practices must be completed in gradual stages. However, we can be flexible in the arrangement of practices. Some may begin with Guru Yoga and follow with Ekagrata Yoga [One-pointedness Meditation], and continue with the ignition of psychic heat practice and so forth. Others who have more time at their disposal may perform all three practices in a single meditation session. You can choose whatever practices and arrangement you wish, but we must still regard the Guru Yoga as the most important.

The practitioner should view his guru as being indivisible from the buddha. When invoking the presence of the Padmakumara Vajra Guru, Master Practitioner of the Secret Teachings, one must say the following three recitations:

Homage to the constantly abiding dharmakaya, the thusness of the three times, the Maha Twin Lotus Ponds, the White-robed Chief Deity Padmakumara.

Homage to the pure sambhogakaya, the thusness of space, the one with perfect radiant features, the White-robed Chief Deity Padmakumara.

Homage to the transforming nirmanakaya, the Infinite Wonderful Dharma, the Holy Red Crown Vajra Guru Padmakumara.

A disciple who cultivated Guru Yoga suddenly saw the guru arriving on a cloud during his meditation. The guru held a white lotus in his hand and descended gradually, passing the lotus to the disciple, who was in meditative absorption. Then he disappeared immediately.

Another individual had prayed for the guru's blessings. In his meditation, he saw the guru riding on a huge elephant with six tusks, and saw his hand holding a pen that was used to write the Sanskrit letters of the Green Tara Mantra in the air. The guru recited every syllable of the Green Tara Mantra, teaching the practitioner until he remembered it. Once the mantra was learned, the guru disappeared and the disciple was overwhelmed with tears of joy.

Another disciple had prayed for the guru's blessings and during his meditation, he saw the guru's facial and bodily features transform into a three-headed, six-armed statue that was several stories tall. The statue was holding dharma implements. His faces displayed a wrathful look, and his body was engulfed by tongue-like flames. His eyes had a piercing and electrifying stare that even the disciple could not look at them directly. Subsequently, the disciple felt remorse. He had committed acts of misconduct that resulted in the guru's manifestation, in a wrathful form, as a warning. During his meditation, he could feel the ground trembling so much that he could not even sit still and fell on the floor. Later, he wrote a letter of repentance.

Another individual had prayed for the guru's blessings. This disciple was suffering from an illness and had come down with a high fever. He suddenly saw the guru approaching, holding a bottle of nectar in his hand which was poured into his body through his crown, curing him of his high fever. He saw his guru touching his head with his hands and felt a surge of gratitude filling his heart, that left him in tears. This disciple, who was suffering from high fever, felt a cool and refreshing rush in his body when the nectar entered his head. He recovered completely the next day.

Another individual had prayed for the guru's blessings in his forty-nine day practices. On the forty-ninth day of his meditation, he suddenly felt a shaft of white light that descended from the sky. In an instant he experienced a clear vision of all things. His body and mind were transformed into white light, and he experienced a sudden increase in wisdom. What he had not understood in the past suddenly made sense to him. He was a different dharma student. In the past, he faced difficulties in each step of his dharma study. Since receiving the blessings of the guru, he gained yogic union through the path of Dharma. He felt the constant presence of his guru, enjoyed a sense of lightness in his body and mind, and found joy that he had never experienced before. The teachings, which were once incomprehensible to him, were now accessible, and he could apply them to his life.

He made three major vows:

1. He would make an offering to his guru every month without fail.
2. He would practice a total of 108 sessions of the Ksitigarbha Deliverance that was transmitted to him by the guru, to liberate spirits in the netherworld.
3. He would become a great dharma protector for his guru, and revered the guru as a buddha. He vowed to follow the guru in all future lives.

One disciple had prayed for the guru's blessings. He had an experience in which he witnessed spots of white, red, green, yellow and blue colored lights that were the size of medicine pills. The disciple was amazed because the appearance of medicine in space corresponded with the disciple's practice of the Medicine Buddha Yoga. The medicine circled three times in space before falling into his hands. Ever since then, the patients who received help from him through the Medicine Buddha Yoga were healed from their illnesses. He was overjoyed and wrote a letter to inform me of this occurrence. Actually I knew about it long before he wrote the letter.

There was a disciple who practiced Guru Yoga diligently but he was ridiculed by a Vajrayana practitioner from a different order. Once, the practitioner slandered me in front of my disciple, and in defense, my disciple said, "Master Sheng-yen Lu is the Lion King Vajra. He is a master who has attained the supreme perfect enlightenment. How dare you insult my guru! If my guru were false, you would certainly have no sin. But if my guru is a genuine one, try insulting him forty-nine times and you may receive retribution at once."

The practitioner laughed out loud and condemned me, repeating, "Sheng-yen Lu is a false master" forty-nine times. Upon completion, he retaliated by asking, "So, where is my retribution?" My disciple left in silence. Three months later, the same practitioner went to a friend's place, which happened to be a timber factory. A crane was picking up a huge log, which accidentally struck the practitioner as it rotated. The practitioner instantly vomited blood and died later at his home. This incident happened in Malaysia.

A disciple had requested the blessings of the guru and in his meditation, he saw many gods entering into his meditation room, encircling him one after another. Subsequently a god in golden armor came and said to the rest of the gods, "Master Sheng-yen Lu has arrived in the sky above." The gods looked up and saw white light illuminating the sky, which was as bright as a lightning flash. Upon closer examination, they saw the guru appearing with a gold body, seated on a lotus throne and emitting the aura light from his crown. Then the assembly of gods placed their palms together in respect and uttered their praise, "In this universal great dharma affinity we shall take refuge. We, the dragons and gods, are willing to protect the Dharma."

After these beings spoke, a thunderclap was heard. At once, the beings ascended into the air. They had red spots on their bodies, along with white bellies and large massive jaws. All in all, there were nine dragons that danced in the sky. The golden armored god rode on one of the dragons and paid homage to the guru. My disciple was astonished to witness this vision and gained even greater reverence for his guru.

There was one disciple who went into the mountains to cultivate Guru Yoga. He found a cave and sat crossed-legged to practice. His residence was in Sumatra, and he lived on a mountain where tigers roamed. Later, a tiger appeared and its presence sent fear into the heart of my disciple. The tiger stared at him while he was seated, and his mind ran wild. He shouted, "Guru save me!" Upon hearing that, the tiger was taken aback by the sound, lowered its head, and made some growling noises before turning away. The disciple immediately ran down the mountain in the cloak of darkness. By shouting "Guru save me," the tiger was frightened away!

One disciple was very respectful of the guru, and he prayed for the guru's blessings in his daily practice. He was a famous artist and painted a huge painting of the guru that could fill an entire wall. On the day of its completion, he hung the painting on his wall and lit a stick of high quality incense. As the smoke from the incense rose to the level of the guru's face, it stopped rising and circulated around the guru's face for about five minutes before dissipating.

On that very night, the artist dreamt that the guru took him to the artist's backyard. The guru pointed to a spot beneath the wall before disappearing into space. The next day, at the same spot, he unearthed a huge box that contained many Vajrayana practice texts, ritual objects, and a piece of a dharma robe. Upon investigating his family history, he found out that his great grandfather had been a great adept of the Vajrayana teachings and had studied Tibetan Buddhism under [an earlier reincarnation of] Tai Situ Rinpoche, from whom he had received His Holiness' dharma robe. Before he passed away, he was concerned that the ritual objects and practice texts might be mistreated, so he decided to place them in a box and bury them underground. Because his present day descendent had taken refuge in Tibetan Buddhism, the ritual objects therefore reemerged. Among the practice texts that he found, one of them was a major practice that was extremely rare and precious.

Another practitioner, who belonged to the Nyingma order, had practiced for many years. He himself was a master. He cultivated the Black Retreat, and practiced the Guanyin [Chenrezig] Yoga. When he attained yogic union, he saw Guanyin Bodhisattva informing him that a Mahasiddha had appeared, and he was none other than Master Sheng-yen Lu. The bodhisattva urged him to take refuge in Master Lu and learn the Dharma from him. This Nyingma master had learned of Sheng-yen Lu's fame earlier, but he was unconvinced of his attainment. Thus, one can imagine his astonishment when the bodhisattva told him about Master Lu.

After coming out of his retreat, this master did not come to look for me immediately. He was already eighty years old, while I am still in my forties. He is a senior master and I am a junior master. Yet, one night, he sat in meditation and heard the Tara's mantra resonating all around him. He saw himself transforming into the face of a baby held in his mother's embrace. When he looked at his mother's face, he was shocked to see the face of Master Sheng-yen Lu. At this point, he had a realization, and decided to put aside the differences of seniority and age, and wrote to seek refuge and empowerment.

Another disciple insisted on gaining yogic response with the guru's statue. Yet, for a long time nothing had happened. He already purchased a statue of the guru for himself, and purchased a few others for those who couldn't afford one. Despite this, he received no spiritual responses.

Then one night, he dreamt of his guru touching his crown and pulling something out of his head with his hand. Finally, the guru pulled a long black worm out of his head, and told him that the black worm of karma had prevented him from receiving any yogic union. The guru informed him that the following day his practice would definitely yield results.

True enough, on the following day, he saw white light entering his crown, and there was a clear path from his navel to the crown. Spiritual vitality filled his entire being. This disciple was able to gain penetration into all Vajrayana teachings, and could transform his crystal clear heart into the form of a lotus flower. He received many major Vajrayana practices and gained yogic union with all of them. Amazingly, he accomplished the Phowa Yoga and could help others open the pathway to the crown chakra.

These are just a few examples to illustrate the spiritual power of the guru's blessings on Mahamudra. I hope all disciples will practice in accordance to these instructions. I am sure that you will all have great accomplishments.

8. Ekagrata Meditation

Once, the Sixteen Gyalwa Karmapa taught me, "Most people that practice meditative absorption find that they cannot still their minds. Their biggest dilemma is that their minds constantly waver back and forth. Thus, we should adopt the Seven-Point Posture of Vairocana, regulate our breathing, and practice the Ekagrata or One-Pointedness Meditation. This approach helps to focus the mind, so that it does not stray away. Thus it helps one enter into meditative absorption easily."

The approach of the Sixteen Gyalwa Karmapa includes three other steps:

> Contemplate on a buddha statue with our eyes. A buddha image is the most adorned form of purity. Whether the image is carved or painted, he is displayed in golden brilliance, an achievement through his meritorious actions, and his face emanates only compassion. His body, which is dressed in three robes and adorned with pearls and jade necklaces, is encircled with halos of light. When we single-mindedly contemplate on the magnificence of the buddha's image, we are practicing Ekagrata or One-Pointedness focus on the buddha's

form. When we do this practice repeatedly over time, the image of the buddha stays constantly in our minds, and we will quickly attain the Purity of One-Pointedness.

Contemplate on the moon disc with our eyes - The crown of the buddha is often seen with the aura of a moon disc. We can focus on this light, for the moon disc symbolizes the gradual elimination of ignorance. The moon waxes and wanes, changing from a crescent to a full moon, which represents the cleansing of all dark karma. On the moon disc, there is usually inscribed the Sanskrit syllable HUM, which represents our self-nature and Buddha-nature. The light of the moon disc originates from the syllable HUM. When we focus our eyes on the light of the moon disc, we constantly think of this light shining upon us, entering through our crown chakra and filling us with pure light. As we constantly contemplate on this light, we attain the Purity of One-Pointedness in no time.

Contemplate on the seeds [relics] with our eyes - Most living buddhas who enter nirvana leave behind many relics or sariras after their cremation. These relics, which are bean-like or oval-shaped and resemble a limestone egg, come in different hues. The Tibetan tulkus, or living buddhas, consider these objects as "seeds." Tibetans are convinced that such objects are evidence of someone attaining sacred power and realizing his true nature. They are symbolic proof of the appearance of the truth body [dharmakaya] from the emanation body [nirmanakaya]. When we place these colored relics in front of us and contemplate on their radiance, that emits pure lights into our hearts, over time we shall attain the Purity of One-Pointedness.

These three kinds of contemplation are:

The sacred contemplation practice.

The light contemplation practice.

The seed contemplation practice.

I have been practicing Mahamudra for many years. Once, I met a teacher who taught me one particular method. In this practice, the practitioner installs a large mirror in front of where one usually sits in meditation, or wherever it is suitable. The mirror should reflect one's whole body so that the practitioner can closely examine oneself. For example, when one is joyous, one should observe one's smile and the happiness on one's face. However, when one receives insults and slander, one's face will naturally reflect unhappiness. These expressions of joy, anger, sadness, and happiness can be observed closely in the mirror. When the facial features are examined closely, one is able to discern the varied facial features, and the changes in expression as they develop each day. In principle, this contemplation is a form of self-reflection, that is also taught in Confucianism in which one sits still to constantly reflect on one's misdeeds. However, in this case, a mirror is hung in front of one to examine one's faults closely. This is similar to how others see us, and hence how we may look at ourselves.

In this respect, when we constantly reflect upon ourselves and observe ourselves, we shall understand the delusion of how others perceive us and how others attach to us. In this way, we achieve the goal of breaking foolish grasping to our illusory physical bodies. This approach of installing a mirror to observe ourselves, helps us to recognize the fact that we are products of illusion that are no different from clouds and smoke, the reflection of the moon in water, an illusory dream, or a reflection of a flower in a mirror. When we achieve this state of Ekagrata or One-Pointedness, we attain the three contemplations of Void, Illusion, and the Middle Way.

When I was studying Taoism, my teacher, Taoist Master Qingzhen of the Qingcheng Sect, secretly taught me a method. His method starts with lighting up two sticks of incense that are about two-and-half feet directly away from one's left and right eyes. Next, with eyes half closed, one rests on a cushion and stares at the burning red tips of the incense. Gradually, one can imprint the red tip image in one's spiritual eye [the inner vision at the center of our head]. I feel that this method is very efficient because as our eyes lock onto the red tips of the brightly glowing incense, the image merges into one spot at the center of the spiritual eye. At this stage, a tingling sensation is felt around the spiritual eye, followed by a feeling of firmness in the area. All of our senses become concentrated at the spiritual eye, which corresponds with the key to mastering the "Major Practice of Meditation on Attaining Realization through the Spiritual Eye."

I have been practicing this method of concentration for many years, and it is a wonderful approach to focus the mind. Ekagrata Meditation can be performed according to one's preferences. If you feel that a certain approach suits you better, then you should adopt that practice, so long as you achieve the goal of focusing the mind with self-control. If one is not interested in Ekagrata, then it would be a fallacy for one to claim that one has attained the Way. If an individual has not cultivated One-Pointedness Meditation, then one's mind would be subject to the influence of one's impure consciousness. One's mind will fluctuate like waves in the great ocean that do not have a moment of peace or tranquility. One's mind will be like a pail of water contaminated with color pigments and sewage that can never become clear. Thus, if a person cultivates the Way with a defiled mind, he will never attain anything.

The difference between the mundane mind and sacred mind is that the mundane mind tends to fluctuate, whereas the sacred mind is tranquil. The mundane mind is constantly engaged in discursive thoughts, craving wealth and sex only. In this way, the individual is constantly losing essence and vitality until old age and death. He or she is consumed with negative karma that draws him or her to the realms of hell, hungry ghosts, or animals. Mahamudra, on the other hand, helps one to realize one's self-nature. It raises the psychic heat, holds the mind in contemplation and stills the thoughts. Hence, it is a supreme practice that constantly turns the dharma wheel.

When a cultivator practices the Ekagrata Meditation, he or she eventually can reveal the "light of original nature." It is like the moon's reflection in clear water, untouched by all things and uncontaminated. One arrives at a point of unattachment to all external conditions, and one achieves the state of non-arising of thoughts.

At this time, there is no contamination arising from the six faculties of eyes, ears, nose, tongue, body and mind, and one's self-nature is untouched by the senses of sight, sound, smell, taste, touch and thought. Though a cultivator's physical body may be in the world, he or she is not bound to the world. Thus, one abandons the perceptions of a self, a being, a life, or a soul. When one reaches this spiritual state, that which is considered the sun, moon, and stars are non-existent to one, and experiences of human emotions are non-existent as well. When all phenomena cease to exist, one is close to attaining the great state of absorption.

When a cultivator practices One-Pointed Meditation, he works on focusing his mind. As the cultivator concentrates on one-point, the circulation of the qi or energy in the channels travel like an electrical current which feels like a pulse. This is called 'qi ling' or 'the awakening of spirit' [translator's note: also known commonly as Kundalini Awakening]. If we learn to gain control over this process, then this spiritual current will definitely help to strengthen our body and cure us of illnesses. Thus, it certainly benefits us greatly. However, if we cannot achieve self-control, we will easily be subject to outside influences and be drawn into a psychotic state of mind. Therefore, it is my wish that anyone who practices this method should maintain a normal diet and have sufficient sleep. If you practice "the awakening of spirit" method to strengthen your physical body, then you should uphold a daily routine with each session lasting no more than twenty minutes. Do not over-exert yourself and do not crave spiritual powers. Then you shall have few worries.

When we practice Ekagrata Meditation and maintain our focus, spiritual experiences are likely to occur. If we do not experience the awakening of spirit, then we may experience various illusory visions and states in our absorption. These visions may arise non-stop. The practitioner may report these illusory visions to his guru and the guru, who is experienced with such conditions, will properly guide and instruct the practitioner with the best solution. You may also choose to completely ignore these visions and focus solely on absorption, remaining unaffected by the visions. When you are unafraid, unworried, and unattached to these visions, you will naturally have no problems. If you are drawn and led by these illusory visions, it is highly probable that you will stray into the mara realms.

When a person sits for too long in the Seven-Point Posture of Vairocana in the practice of Mahamudra, one's body and mind may become fatigued, and one may tend to doze off and enter into a dream state. If one knows how to awaken one's spirit, then one may move one's body automatically to counter the sleepiness. If one does not know the art of awakening the spirit, then one should spend time climbing, enjoying the ocean, or looking at some picturesque sceneries to allow the body and mind to recuperate from fatigue. When our mind is comfortable, it is easier to enter into absorption. These are important points to take note of.

Ekagrata or One-Pointedness, can help one to reach the bliss of oneness of mind. Thus, it is a state of immovability, which reaches into the realm of nirvana. The teachings in my book, *The Illuminated Way of Meditation* [Book 45], are within the scope of Ekagrata Meditation. If one masters the meditation in the book, one will transcend the heavenly realm as well as the three realms. One will be in a state of birthlessness and deathlessness. It is certainly powerful.

Mahamudra is thus a unified practice, combining all practices. It is cultivated in stages before one reaches great attainment. By practicing Ekagrata, one attains purity of body, speech and mind, which together constitutes the supreme state of meditative absorption.

The secret of Vajrayana lies in achieving yogic union, so success really hinges on the accuracy of the tool or mantra being used.

Sheng-yen Lu

9. Circulation of Mantra and Breathing

The highest practice of the Kagyu School of Tibetan Buddhism is the practice of Mahamudra.

One Mahamudra mantra is: "Om so-ba-wa su-da sa-er-wa, da-er-ma so-ba-wa su-do-hang" [also known as the Emptiness Visualization Mantra]. The meaning of this mantra is purity of self-nature and purity of the nature of all phenomena. This Mahamudra mantra is most perfect, and we should memorize it and recite it often.

Mantras are often recited using the Vajra Recitation Method (secret recitation), also termed as *vajrajapa*, which means silence.

I have been studying mantras for many years, and my teachers include Tibetans and Chinese. I find that the pronunciations of mantras are truly diverse and confusing, since each teacher has his or her own unique accent. Take, for example, the Chinese language. Sichuan Chinese, Beijing Chinese, Shandong Chinese, and Fujian Chinese are all very different from each other.

It is the same in Tibet, where many local accents are found. In Nepal, the Himalayas region, the snow mountains region, Tibet (*Utsang* - front Tibet or *Tsang* - rear Tibet), Kashmir, Punjab, Sikkim, Bhutan, Assam, and Uttar Pradesh, many languages are spoken within a single region, and there are so many regions. To my knowledge, in the Himalayas there are over twenty different languages spoken by various ethnic groups.

How does one obtain the correct pronunciation of the mantras? I feel that practitioners should adhere to the pronunciation as transmitted by their own guru, and avoid learning too many variations of mantras. Once a person learns many forms of pronunciation, one may be lost and confused as to which version is correct, and as a result, one may lose one's faith in reciting mantra.

There is a person called Lai Shih-pei who lives in California, USA. He sent me a book entitled *Correct Sanskrit Mantras*, which was printed by the Mahayana Sutra Publisher in Taiwan.

In the preface, Lai Shih-pei wrote, "Mantras, as transmitted in Vajrayana Buddhism, are genuine dharma treasures which are directly realized by all buddhas." They are the main tools used in cultivation. The secret of Vajrayana lies in achieving yogic union, so success really hinges on the accuracy of the tool or mantra being used. Most pronunciations of mantras today have departed from their original pronunciations and have lost their accuracy. This is why it is so difficult for cultivators to achieve any response from their cultivation, and why they sometimes need to work twice as hard to achieve the same results. Even if they rely on Tibetan phonetics, their pronunciation is not the same as the original source.

In order to resolve this issue, I strived to find a descendent from the Brahmin caste in Nepal. The Brahmins are taught to recite the ancient Sanskrit literature since childhood, so this person was an authority on pronunciation. His academic achievement included a Doctoral Degree in Sanskrit Studies. Thus, in a joint venture, we made transliterations and recordings of the mantras from the Buddhist Canon (Tripitaka), and offer the following as a reference for practitioners. The Sanskrit mantras include:

1. The thirty-four commonly used minor mantras
2. The Great Compassion Dharani
3. *Guhyasamaja Tantra*
4. *Hevajra Tantra*
5. Dharani of Mahapratisara-vidyarajn
6. Root Sadhana of Universal-Prevailing Manjusri
7. *Sutra of the Great Thousand Defender of the Land*
8. *Mahamayuri-vidyarajni Sutra*

This book was edited and compiled by Mr. Lai Shih-pei, and a great deal of effort went into the work. It was published by the Mahayana Sutra Publisher. After listening to the audio cassette recording of the mantra recitation, I invited the resident lamas at the Washington Center of Tibetan Language to listen to the tape, and they commented that the mantras were delivered with proper pronunciation. If you are interested in the correct pronunciation of mantras, you may refer to the Mahayana Sutra Publisher.

So far, the pronunciation of mantras has been discussed.

In regards to the mantra and breathing practices of Mahamudra, they involve the exchange and circulation of winds. This is one of the Mahamudra secrets. When one is practicing breathing in Mahamudra, the nutrients in the winds are absorbed into the body and directly into the bloodstream. It is not absorbed through the lungs. This flow of winds enters and circulates within the mind and body. When one is inhaling, one visualizes the winds as "pure and clear," and when one is exhaling, one visualizes "impurities." In principle, we apply the complete breathing method, where the inhalation is slow and drawn out, followed by a similarly slow exhalation. This is known as the Turtle Breathing Method.

We visualize the body as composed of these five elements:

> Our heart, lungs and kidneys originate from and are made up of the earth element.

Our blood and fluids originate from and are made up of the water element.

The heat from our bodies originate from and are made up of the fire element.

Our breath originates from and are made up of the wind element.

The human body is formed from these four illusory elements. In times of illness, the four elements are in disharmony and upon death, the four elements are dispersed.

In addition, the unique spiritual nature inherent in the human body, which is referred to as the "soul," is wonderous and subtle. This is the space element.

Regarding the recitation of mantras and breathing visualizations, a novice is required to visualize according to the methods mentioned above. However, the visualizations are practiced differently by an enlightened adept.

The novice practitioner inhales the pure white seed syllable OM, and exhales the blue seed syllable HUM. When the breath abides in the body, it takes the form of the red seed syllable AH.

The enlightened adept; however, inhales the blue seed syllable HUM and exhales the white syllable OM. When the breath abides in the body, it takes the form of the red seed syllable AH.

What is happening here? The physical body of the novice Mahamudra practitioner is still filled with karmic hindrances. Thus, it is necessary to inhale light and exhale filthy energy. On the contrary, an enlightened adept seeks to deliver sentient beings, so the adept inhales the filthy energy of beings and suffers on their behalf. He, in turn, exhales the breath of light to be absorbed by sentient beings. The Tibetans believe that if one breathes in even a little of the breath exhaled by a great yogi, one will benefit from it because the breath of the adept can eliminate karmic hindrances and heal sicknesses.

The syllable HUM does not necessarily represent filthy energy. It is a symbol of the blue sky, which represents the manifested power of buddhas and bodhisattvas. The syllable HUM can also be considered as an emanation of Sakyamuni and the buddhas and bodhisattvas, whose spiritual power is so strong that it vibrates throughout the world. OM embodies white light, AH embodies red light, and HUM embodies blue light. When we breath, we need to visualize the seed syllables in detail. I want to state that OM is the pure clear light, AH is the psychic heat, and HUM is the spiritual power.

The wind of white pure light is inhaled gently through the nose until it fills in the lungs, blood, fluids, dantian [an area four inches below the navel] and eventually the whole body. Some practitioners may practice the yoga of visualizing the breath and the dantian in the shape of a vase. To do this, hold your breath temporarily within your body for as long as you can, and then exhale gradually through the nose. This approach of combining the use of mantra and breath is known as Mahamudra.

The combination of mantra, thought and breath is one of the greatest secret methods hidden in the cosmos.. While it is true that our discursive thoughts are distractive, as long as we can maintain our practice using mantra, thought and breath, our discursive thoughts will naturally become still. Our mind will naturally be in tune with the realm of suchness. These three elements of mantra, thought and breath, blend and work together.

Someone once asked me what counts as a single cycle of breathing? This is how I count: As I inhale, I count six beats and then hold for two beats. As I exhale, I count six beats and then pause for two beats. According to the Tibetan lamas, there are approximately twenty-one thousand and six-hundred breathing cycles in a twenty four-hour period. This works out to be nine-hundred breathing cycles per hour, or fifteen breathing cycles per minute. This is what the lamas consider to be the standard number of breathing cycles in a day.

The veil of Mahamudra is gradually lifted as my writing progresses to this stage. I, the Holy Red Crown Vajra Guru Sheng-yen Lu, Venerable Lian-sheng, am not the kind of person who makes empty promises. I am a true practitioner who speaks honestly, and a master who has gained realization. I have attained yogic response and I am a buddha. I can become one with the supreme cosmic consciousness in an instant, and receive the blessings of supreme and wonderful treasures of adornment. I am one with all past lineage holders.

This is the emergence of the highest teachings in the world. I have indeed attained all cosmic and inner secrets.

10. Techniques of Mahamudra

After moving to Seattle, USA, I continued vigorously with my daily cultivation. Besides entering into meditative absorption, I also practiced Mahamudra techniques. These techniques, known as Asanas, are essential. What are the techniques of Mahamudra? They are a set of techniques that are exercised to compliment the meditation of Mahamudra. Each of the seven chakras that we will discuss below is "a plexus of nerves," which constitute the meridians. As we direct winds into the meridians, we must release the knots in the meridians.

If a practitioner of Mahamudra increases their spiritual strength, yet their physical body is weak, then this results in an imbalance. Exercising with these techniques contributes to the development of balance in the body, mind and spirit. The meditative absorption of Mahamudra and the physical techniques of Mahamudra compliment each other.

The Sixteen Gyalwa Karmapa once transmitted a technique to me known as the Vajra Techniques of Great Bliss. In the past, I learned many other techniques from other yogis. Thus, the vajra techniques I am about to introduce are rather eclectic. I want to teach you a few simple techniques that can be done easily. While they may appear simple and easy, they are nevertheless significant. The students must first pay homage to the guru and lineage holders to show respect.

The physical techniques of Mahamudra are as follows:

1. *The Life Force Technique* [Resembles the Forward Bend Posture or the Paschimothanasana]

From a lying position, with your arms straight out behind you, inhale slowly and lift your upper body slowly from your waist. Then continue to bend forward, lowering your upper body as far as you can and grasp your toes with your fingers. Hold your breath for 3 to 8 seconds before releasing it. Bend backwards until you are lying flat on your back. Repeat this sequence 8 times.

This technique resembles the exercise of a sit-up, but it differs slightly. One may visualize white light while inhaling, blue light while exhaling, and red light while holding the breath. The breathing should be gradual and full. The body should bend and extend from the waist from as low of a point as possible, ideally resting the chest on the thighs.

This Life Force Technique helps to press the winds toward the solar plexus chakra [located a few inches above the navel], so as to release all the knots around that chakra.

2. *The Loosening Technique*

Seated in the cross-legged full lotus position, with the hands clasped in a fist and held closely at the waist, turn the upper body from right to left and from left to right in one sequence. Repeat this five times. Turning the body this way helps to loosen the knots around the solar plexus chakra, which helps to clear the knots and eliminate any problems in the navel area.

3. *The Inversion Technique* [Resembles the Supported Shoulder Stand or Salamba-Sarvangasana]

This is an inverted pose. The novice may learn it by supporting himself against a wall. This inverted pose requires the head, neck and shoulder areas to be on the floor, with the hands placed on the spine to support the back, while keeping the elbows in and resting on the floor. The body beyond the shoulder forms a straight line. Tuck your chin against your chest and keep your legs together, focusing your attention on the tips of your feet.

Keep your body still. Hold the pose for about 2 to 5 minutes. Repeat 3 times.

This inversion technique serves to fill the body with wind. After completing this technique, rotate your neck several times either clockwise or counter-clockwise to release the knots around the throat chakra. This posture can eliminate problems around the throat chakra.

However, this inversion technique is unsuitable for the elderly and those suffering from high blood pressure. Those who are unable to do a shoulder stand should not attempt this technique.

4. *The Slapping Technique*

This technique requires one to sit cross-legged. Extend your hands and rub your palms to produce heat. Lift your right arm straight up to expose the armpit. Slap your right armpit 3 times with your left palm.

Repeat this with your left arm extending straight up, and slap the left armpit 3 times with your right palm.

Following this, massage your left and right shoulders respectively by rubbing them with your hands. You can combine the techniques of rubbing and slapping. You can even slap your chest area. By slapping from your shoulders down to your legs and feet, including your toes, you are literally giving your body a full slapping massage.

This approach is one of the best ways to loosen the heart chakra and the meridians in the armpit area. Usually, it is difficult for the winds to circulate through the meridians at the armpit; this is a dead end in the practice of Mahamudra. It is just as difficult for the wind to reach the tip of the toes. This is made possible with the force of the slapping technique. This is vital. This technique can cure problems arising around the heart and chest area.

Someone has described this technique as the flapping wings of a bird. You can slap on your arms and hands, and on the area around your chest, waist and legs.

I would like to elucidate on this further: If the "Awakening of Spirit" exercise of the Golden Mother of Jade Pond is performed while fully conscious with a good control of timing, then it is no different from the Slapping Technique mentioned here. By applying the force of slapping, one releases all the knots in the meridians and helps to improve the health of the body. The "Awakening of Spirit" exercise includes the techniques of slapping, rotating and twisting the body. This exercise applies these techniques to cure the illnesses of the body by clearing the knots in the meridians, and helping to circulate the winds within them.

5. *The Light Technique* [Resembles the Virasana or Hero Pose]

This technique involves sitting in a kneeling position. However, the body does not rest on the legs, but the buttocks are seated on the floor between the left and right legs, which are parted and bent backwards, so that the body and the tips of the toes form a ninety degree angle. This applies to both legs. The palms are stretched to touch the kneecaps. This sitting position basically turns the kneecaps. The thighs are kept together, with the left thigh touching the left calf, and the right thigh touching the right calf.

Hold this sitting pose for 30 seconds at a time, and repeat it 4 times. This Light Technique unlocks the knots in the meridians of the knees, and these meridians are among the most difficult to clear. When the knots are released, problems of the lower body shall be removed.

6. *The Shaking Technique*

Many yogins often support the physical body with their hands and then let go, allowing their whole body to hit the floor. This sudden throwing of the body on the floor is said to help loosen the knots of the whole body. Other yogis sit firmly on their buttocks and kick their legs towards the sky, shaking them after kicking. This serves to loosen the knots in the lower body. Some yogins instruct others to do rope skipping for 10 to 30 minutes daily. This is applying the method of trembling, which is intended to loosen the knots.

7. *The Buddha Prostration Technique*

The Buddha Prostration Technique may appear simple, yet it is far from being simple. The technique can heal one from sickness, and also clear the knots in the meridians. Besides, it involves prostration to buddhas. This technique has many benefits.

The method is as follows: First, kneel down so that your buttocks rest on the soles of your feet. Hold your palms together. Inhale and raise your arms upwards towards the sky so that your arms touch your ears. Then prostrate by bending your body forward, with your chest touching your thighs as closely as possible. Stretch your arms forward, and ideally touch your forehead and nose to the floor. At this stage it is important to breathe out all the air in your lungs. Hold yourself in prostration for 8 seconds before inhaling a fresh breath, and then lift your body upwards and repeat the initial sequence. The Buddha Prostration Technique should be performed 9 times in every session. Perhaps the more the merrier.

This technique releases the knots around the solar plexus chakra and eliminates problems around the stomach or waist.

To open all the chakras of the body with the practice of Mahamudra involves pith instructions and techniques. The clearing of each chakra produces great bliss, and leads one to recognize and attain the great inherent wisdom. With the opening of the seven chakras, one naturally enters into samadhi.

The psychic heat circulates within the charkas, which gives rise to unmatched vibration. This psychic heat permeates the whole body, rendering it in flames, reaching the level in which every outward breath can fill the space of the universe. One who attains this level of accomplishment naturally finds a protrusion on the top of one's crown, like those seen on buddhas and bodhisattvas. At this stage, the individual has attained the great vajra body and knows what it is like to truly be in the supreme victorious realm of attainment. As I pen these words, I cannot help but sigh over the ignorance of sentient beings who are oblivious to cultivation, and are thus completely un-aware of the greatness of accomplishment attained through the prac-tice of Mahamudra!

11. Dual Use of Tranquility and Contemplation

What is tranquility [*samatha*]? Tranquility is concentration. What is contemplation [*vipasyana*]? Contemplation is wisdom.

The method of applying tranquility and contemplation serves to calm and eliminate discursive thoughts. As a result, one achieves the stage where one gains wisdom through contemplating that all things are inherently empty, that all things are illusory and temporary, and that all things lie in the Middle Way.

That is why Tientai School is also known as Zhiguan School, because the school's main practice is tranquility [zhi in Chinese] and contemplation [guan in Chinese].

What is generally known as Ten Contemplations or Ten Views are contemplations on the following: emotional afflictions, the netherworld, karmic obscurations, illnesses, meditative absorption, mara interferences, ego and arrogance, diverse views, views of bodhisattvas, and views of the two vehicles. The dual functioning of tranquility and contemplation corresponds to the dual use of concentration and wisdom.

There is a [recreation area] called Carkeek Park, located in northwest Seattle, adjacent to the Pacific Ocean. I love to relax there and listen to the ocean's sound. Watching the turquoise ocean swaying like a gigantic bed under the blue sky, I am totally fascinated by the magic of nature. The ocean ripples endlessly, constantly renewing itself. How much do we as humans know about the ocean? Who is able to understand it?

The ocean speaks out loud like roaring thunder. However, I know that it is not the sound of the ocean, but the voice of life. At times, the sound is soft, resembling that of a tender hand. Other times, it seems to laugh out of mockery, scorning the foolishness of humans. Sometimes the ocean is upset, crying angrily like the galloping of thousands of horses. Sometimes it murmurs, longing for its wounds to heal because it was hurt countless times. The ocean is a great cosmos, expressing itself in infinite forms, while being endowed with endless causes and effects, endless thoughts, and endless sounds.

I like to look at the ocean and listen to its roar, to think and contemplate on it, for the ocean holds water from all rivers in one place, summing up the collective emotions in one single body. The rivers are always flowing, unlike the ocean, which collects all thoughts, pains, desperation, dependencies, wounds, and numerous desires.

In the quiescence of my meditation, I hear the ocean reciting mantras. The sound of the rolling waves signifies the pinnacle of all mantras, for the ocean is repeatedly chanting the syllable "OM, OM, OM," which supersedes all other mantra sounds. The ocean is one with all things, and I am one with the ocean. Everything in the universe is united in one body of life, existing in perfect harmony.

I have understood the meaning of tranquility and contemplation. My heart is in tune with the ocean. Even though all of my books are imprinted in my mind, they also resemble the ocean expressing themselves in myriads of manifestations. The ocean rests, flows, re-emerges, and changes its forms ceaselessly. What is the true reality of my being? Is it the nirvana of the Buddha, or the union of sacredness, sensitivities, or divinities?

I have come to understand everything, and the ocean has taught me to create wondrous things with great wisdom. If the readers can truly understand the ocean language that I am trying to convey, they have reached the maturity of comprehension. They comprehend the heart essence of the dual use of tranquility and contemplation.

The Mahamudra practice of tranquility and contemplation involves three levels:

1. Cutting all thoughts instantly.
2. Unleashing the stream of thoughts and allowing them to run wild without attempting to stop them.
3. Letting the thoughts run alongside the mind, watching them pass by like a flowing stream of water.

During meditative absorption, we must first sever discursive thoughts to avoid distraction and disturbance. When a single thought arises, we must cut it away at once. This is the first key to practicing meditative absorption, which is also the first stage of cutting discursive thoughts.

However, the meditator will eventually realize that it is fruitless to eliminate thoughts, as the attempt to avoid them will just trigger more to arise. Ensuing thoughts come fast and furious, without a moment of rest, just the way a turbulent river rises and rolls incessantly. When one arrives at this stage, it is best to simply let the thoughts flow without attempting to still them. This constitutes the second stage.

Upon arriving at the third stage, the Mahamudra practitioner, while in meditative absorption, must visualize all thoughts like a flowing river. The practitioner sits beside the river and allows them to flow past. While the thoughts keep flowing, the practitioner observes them in stillness without being affected by them. When the practitioner manages to depart from his or her thoughts and becomes an observer of the steaming thoughts, the mind achieves self-mastery and reaches the realm of true reality.

The first spiritual stage is severing the thoughts when they arise. This is tranquility.

The second spiritual stage is allowing the thoughts to wander without attempting to stop the thought stream. This is letting them be, which is being natural.

The third spiritual stage is going beyond the thoughts, and standing beside the thought stream without clinging to it. This is contemplation.

The core of Mahamudra meditation is to train the individual to abide continuously in the quiescence of the third spiritual stage. It is a world of complete purity that is free from worries because one is unaffected by the influence of wandering thoughts. The sage who arrives at this spiritual state finds that the mind is constantly abiding in an unchanging spiritual realm. Regardless of the changes in the environment, the sage is able to apply both tranquility and contemplation, through which he or she attains realization and maintains the state of nirvana.

The following explanations are based on my experience:

The first spiritual stage is too tight, where the controlling of thoughts is overly restrictive, and the mind becomes stubborn.

The second spiritual stage is too lax, where the mind becomes lazy and uncontrollable.

The third spiritual stage constitutes balance, where one stops thinking at times but also contemplates at times. This is the dual use of tranquility and contemplation, where the mixed way of tightening and loosening is the dual functioning of concentration and wisdom. To separate the mind from thoughts is an important key because one will make great gains in spiritual advancement if one trains the mind in this way.

I have studied the Three Contemplations of the Tientai School.

Those concepts are known by many names. Some call them the "Three Perfect Contemplations," while others call them the "Three Incomprehensible Contemplations." Some also refer to them as the "Three Non-Procedural Contemplations." The Three Contemplations are further explained as the following: Contemplating on emptiness to eliminate delusions arising from incorrect views and thoughts to attain prajna or wisdom. By contemplating on the temporary nature of all phenomena, numerous delusions that hinder knowledge will be eliminated. Furthermore, one will attain the wisdom of skillful means and gain liberation. By contemplating on the Middle Way, delusions arising from ignorance will be eliminated. Furthermore, one will attain the all-inclusive wisdom and gain the virtues of the dharmakaya [truth body]. The three contemplations can be defined respectively as the Three Contemplations of Tiantai School, the Three Contemplations of the Avatamsaka School, the Three Contemplations of the Southern Mountain, and the Three Contemplations of Gratitude. Whether it is through the all-knowing wisdom that understands the principle of emptiness, the wisdom of skillful means that penetrates all phenomena, or the all-inclusive wisdom that observes the Middle Way, eventually all three wisdoms will arise simultaneously, representing the union of emptiness, phenomena, and the Middle Way.

The dual use of tranquility and contemplation is a foremost essential teaching of Vajrayana. It is also the quintessence of yoga practice in India. During the Northern Qi Dynasty [550-577 CE] in China, Master Huiwen learned the practice and taught it to Master Huisi, who passed the dharma torch to Master Zhiyi. Through the continuous transmission, the teachings flourished. Subsequently, the Tientai School established its status through the teaching of One Perfect Contemplation, and became the patriarch of tranquility and contemplation.

Master Zhiyi combined and integrated the principles of emptiness, phenomena, and the Middle Way into one. Then, he destroyed the

delusions arising from incorrect views, provisional existence and ignorance, which gave rise to the wisdom of all-knowing [wisdom of
the sravaka and pratyeka-buddha], the wisdom of skillful means [the
wisdom of bodhisattvas], and the wisdom of all-inclusive cognition
[the wisdom of the buddhas]. Through one mind, the virtues of prajna, liberation, and dharmakaya are thus achieved. This requires one
to perform the dual contemplation on emptiness and phenomena,
through which the meaning of the Middle Way is revealed.

Bodhisattva Nagarjuna's approach was to separate duality to show
the emptiness.

Master Zhiyi's method was to merge duality to introduce the Middle Way.

The philosophy of the Tientai School evolved from a system of
thoughts based on the *Prajnaparamita Sutra*. Many concepts could
only be represented literally, [due to the limited meaning of the lan-
guage]. I think that such abstract concepts are not easily understood
or accepted by most people. Therefore, it was difficult for the teachings to be widely accepted because the readers could not easily comprehend the ideas. I totally understand that although these teachings
may rank as the highest supreme truth, those without actual experience [of practicing the teachings] will not be able to grasp them.

Today, I have clearly elaborated on the dual use of tranquility and
contemplation in this article. I have revealed it from a philosophi-
cal and experiential perspective, so that readers can absorb it quickly.
Master Zhiyi's exposition of the dharma was inconceivable, and my
expounding of his dharma is likewise inconceivable.

I am an accomplished Mahamudra adept who has a superb understanding of wisdom. This is not an attempt to brag about [knowing]
the truth, but it is the very light of wisdom itself.

12. Spiritual State of Supreme Bliss

In this article, I will reveal the secrets of the yab-yum [union of father and mother] buddha statues.

The consort practice is one type of practice within Tibetan Buddhism. Indeed, there are numerous Tibetan buddhist statues displayed in the yab-yum posture, where father and mother buddhas are locked in embrace. The common folk call them the "Buddhas of Pleasure."

Why are they like that? Outsiders are quite puzzled, and even some Vajrayana practitioners don't know either. These Buddhist statues of pleasure have been passed down through the generations, and they continue to remain a mystery in peoples' minds. I have discussed the subject of the consort practice in previous books. Since I am writing about the state of Supreme Bliss of Mahamudra, I have no choice but to reveal the secrets of these yab-yum buddhist statues.

One of the heavenly beings who appears in the yab-yum posture is known by the Sanskrit name as Ganapati, also known as the Lord of Pleasure [Maharya-nandikesvara]. Ganapati was a cunning Brahmin god. As a result, the merciful Guanyin Bodhisattva wanted to direct him to the righteous path, so she transformed herself into a ravishingly beautiful woman to attract him. The Lord of Pleasure was totally captivated by her beauty and was immediately sexually aroused. He wanted to be physically intimate and engage in sexual union with her. At first, Guanyin Bodhisattva refused. Then, she told the Lord of Pleasure that if he wanted to marry her, he must first take refuge in Buddhism and promise to protect the Buddha-dharma. The Lord of Pleasure really wanted to marry her, so he agreed to protect and uphold the Buddha-dharma. The charming lady then smiled and embraced the Lord.

Thus, the image of the Lord of Pleasure is always presented in yab-yum form. In the scripture entitled Deva Form of the Lord of Pleasure, the Yab-Yum Ganesha states, "The yab-yum image of the Lord is depicted with white skin color and he wears a red-colored skirt. The couple is depicted in a standing position and they are locked in embrace. The statue may either be seven or five inches high, with both figures appearing with elephant heads and human bodies. The male deity looks over the right shoulder of the female consort with his eyes gazed at her back, while the female consort leans over the right shoulder of the male figure with her eyes gazed at his back. The legs of the female consort are exposed, and her arms and legs are soft. She is plump in appearance. The male figure's head is adorned with flowers, and he wears a red-colored robe. The head of the female consort is decorated with flowers, and she wears a robe as well. Her arms and legs are adorned with pearls and jade bracelets, and her feet step on the toes of the male. They embrace each other with their arms wrapped around their waists, which reach the backs of their right upper arms.

This consort embrace is recorded in the Buddhist Canon. Why are there so many Vajrayana buddhas, bodhisattvas, and dharma protectors seen in yab-yum union? I shall elucidate on this subject further:

When the light drops and inner fire are generated from the Yoga of Psychic Heat [Tummo], they pass through the seven nerve plexuses, or chakras causing the adept to experience indescribable joy and sensations of bliss that are beyond words. It is very delightful and ethereal, as if one has become an immortal riding on the clouds. The simplest descriptions would be "Becoming a Buddha or an Immortal," "The Great Calm and Joyous Absorption," or "A Spiritual State of Supreme Bliss." This unexcelled state of bliss is absolutely beyond description. Therefore, some compare such bliss to the pleasure experienced during climax when a couple is having sex. The Buddhist statues of pleasure thus illustrate the pinnacle state of Supreme Bliss.

Therefore, the Buddhist statues of pleasure are just symbolic representations of Supreme Bliss, since it is beyond verbal description or depiction in images. The union of men and women are thus figurative expressions of Supreme Bliss. In summary, the yab-yum buddha statues in Tibetan Buddhism are meant to express the contentment from realization upon entering the state of Supreme Bliss.

Yet, many people including some Vajrayana practitioners, have mistakenly assumed that there is a meditative practice for gaining realization through sexual union. Some lamas, in fact, found some beautiful women and embraced them in meditation. This is all fine so long as people don't attempt to do the consort practice. Once people step into the wrong territory, they will indulge themselves in licentiousness and eventually fall down to hell. They only seek physical lust. If cultivators become so lowly and devious, they are on their way to hell and they will meet Mara.

Is there a consort practice in Vajrayana Buddhism? My answer is yes. However, the practice does not require a couple to meditate in sexual embrace. If one emulates the sheer posture of the pleasure statues in their practice, one will commit a grave error. As an enlightened adept, I am certain that the consort practice has nothing to do with the union of a man and woman. Rather, it relates to the yin and yang within us. In fact, there are yin and yang energies, masculine and feminine qualities, and water and fire elements within our body.

The Buddhist pleasure statues actually symbolize the union of yin and yang energies, of masculine and feminine qualities, and of water and fire elements. Attainment of the spiritual state of Supreme Bliss depends on the intangible union of masculine and feminine qualities, rather than the physical embrace of male and female. I hope this explanation helps the readers to gain a clear picture on this matter.

Let me further explain that when a seasoned adept ignites the psychic heat from his root chakra, the heat will rise through the sacral chakra, the solar plexus chakra, the heart chakra, the throat chakra, the third-eye chakra, and eventually reach up to the crown chakra. In terms of visualization, the adept should correspond the psychic heat to the fire element, masculine characteristics, and yang energy. The crown chakra holds the bodhicitta moon nectar or white bindu, which represents the water element and yin energy. The rising of the psychic heat fortifies the yang energy and brings about supreme realization, whereas [the descending of] white bindu strengthens the yin energy and causes supreme wisdom. With the white bindu trickling downwards and the psychic heat traveling upwards, the two merge at each respective chakra, which gives rise to Supreme Bliss. Unfortunately, such bliss is often misinterpreted as the physical pleasure between men and women.

The true consort practice serves to harmonize yin and yang, to unite the masculine and feminine, and to blend water and fire – which can all be attained within one's own body without seeking an actual female partner. Similarly, the Taoist Practice concerning the Male Kan and Female Li also does not require sexual embrace. It also deals with the masculine and feminine elements within one's own body. Many people are led astray by the wrong idea of the consort practice. For example, the Taoist approach of harvesting and supplementing energy [from the opposite sex] is an absolute abuse and it is unethical conduct. Some Vajrayana practitioners see the posture of the pleasure statues, blindly assume that they understand their meaning, and then follow suit. They don't know that the Buddhas of Pleasure actually symbolize the merging of the psychic heat and white bindu. For goodness sakes! There are only a few who truly understand the genuine meaning.

The bliss attained from the Supreme Bliss is not tantamount to that of physical intimacy, nor any other pleasure in the material world. Hence, its name is the spiritual state of Supreme Bliss. Human beings long for happiness. Some obtain it by gathering wealth, while others seek pleasure by gaining power. Some desire to rule the world, while others prefer physical indulgence. In reality, the joys gained from wealth, power, and lust are nothing but short-lived. Take physical pleasure for example. These pleasures are reflective of our animal instincts. Other forms of joy derived from drinking, eating, and touching are temporal. In short, the impermanent joy that humans experience both stem from and are led by our animal instincts.

Yet, the Supreme Bliss attained from the practice of Mahamudra rises from the merging of psychic heat and bodhicitta moon nectar. Once an adept reaches this supreme state, he can truly enter into samadhi, in which his self-nature completely attunes with the eternal bliss of the great universe. This is the true, genuine, and infinite joy.

In my view, all worldly possessions are finite and temporary. Our lives are not eternal, and neither is the earth. The satisfaction of lust, wealth, and power is not everlasting. Only the practitioners who have experienced the Supreme Bliss can truly testify that. Only the supreme consciousness of the universe is eternal and infinite, and only those who partake in this journey of cultivation are genuine masters, true gurus, and are spiritually supreme.

Once the psychic heat arises, how do the drops of white bindu come down? The practitioner must first learn the Yoga of Inner Fire or Psychic Heat, then become well-versed in the full breathing practice, and finally perfect all the techniques in Mahamudra. At this ripe stage, he can visualize the psychic heat rising from the seed syllable AH, flaming up to the crown chakra, and liquefying the solid HAN syllable. As a result, the seed syllable melts and drips downwards. As the white bindu drippings meet the psychic heat at each chakra, they fuse together and fill every single chakra, which gives rise to the spiritual state of Supreme Bliss.

No mundane pleasure can amount to the bliss experienced in this supreme state - the greatest and most wonderful joy. At this time, the mind and spirit abide in the state of self-mastery and void, showered by divine brilliance and pristine joy. Essentially, such bliss can be described by these four words, "great," "uplifting," "sublime," and "divine."

Worldly pleasure is a defiled form of worldly accomplishment.

The spiritual state of Supreme Bliss is a transcendental and untainted accomplishment.

When the Mahamudra practitioner arrives at the Supreme Bliss state, he will be undisturbed and detached from emotions of sadness or happiness. He will realize the illusory nature of phenomena and non-duality of form and emptiness, which worldly people cannot comprehend. In such a supreme state, all things unfold, and the inconceivable joy that stems from good and pure karma will be validated.

I have now revealed the symbolism of the Buddhas of Pleasure and the secrets of consort practice in this article.

13. Spiritual State of Immovability

During the Supreme Bliss state, the winds flow through the channel knots and fan up the [flames of the] psychic heat, which then circulate through the entire body. At this time, mind and matter become a single entity, creating a state of balance and synchronization. The inherent nature of the mind emerges, and divine guidance manifests. This stage is considered the initial stage of samadhi in Mahamudra.

After the initial state, if the practitioner can tune his inherent mind to the supreme consciousness of the cosmos and immerse in the deep state of samadhi, the type of meditative absorption experienced will transform from that of a layman to a sage. If he continues to achieve union even after his inherent mind has totally merged with the universe, then he will attain the ability to transform to any spiritual state at will. If he can remain in this state for an extended period of time, including the moment of his departure, he will be able to unshackle himself from the chain of cyclic existence, achieve Buddhahood in the present body, and reap the fruition of great liberation and release.

In the state of Supreme Bliss, hallucinations may appear when the psychic heat passes through the channel knots. These hallucinations are manufactured by the mara states, causing one to potentially have mental disorders. In the supreme state, one will experience a sensation of lightness, as though one is floating in space. One may even find oneself drifting in an ethereal realm, and then disappearing into the void completely. All forms of illusions and delusions suddenly appear and some practitioners will become enthralled by these hallucinations. As a result, they may generate likes and dislikes, or be attached to taking and giving, which causes them to develop grasping. Once grasping arises, they will fall into the net of the mara states. Thus, it is of vital importance throughout the practice to properly handle the hallucinations.

In most Sutrayana traditions, the secrets of the psychic heat practice are a taboo, due to the fear that most mundane humans are not spiritually steady enough. When individuals reach the supreme state, they may fall into the mara states soon after. Therefore, the teachings in the Sutrayana traditions focus on reciting the buddha's name. The teachings emphasize that by relying on the buddhas and the power of Amitabha Buddha, people will be reborn in the Western Paradise of Ultimate Bliss. After arriving there, people can continue to pursue the path of Buddhahood. This is a safer way to avoid the mara states.

I first studied Taoism, followed by Sutrayana, before I finally settled and focused on Vajrayana. I have been wanting to write the Highest Yoga Tantra and Mahamudra book for quite a while. I mastered the Eighteen Assemblies in the Vajrasekhara [Sutra], and received the full pith teachings and transmissions in the Five Tantras of Garbhadhatu. Thus, I am capable of validating the quintessence of the Three Secrets in Vajrayana. However, I see that the natural capacities in sentient beings are quite far apart. Therefore, I want to emphasize that if anyone is inspired by this book and would like to practice the Highest Yoga Tantra, he must first seek an authentic guru, take refuge in him, and receive the empowerments before starting the practice. People should not blindly dive into the practice without proper guidance from a qualified master. In Tibet, only a few adepts have the high qualifications required to practice Mahamudra. Those who merely show vague curiosity, who have insufficient concentration, or who have weak spiritual energy, are destined to fall into the mara states.

Many Tibetan lamas and Chinese Vajrayana practitioners have reservations about the Highest Yoga Tantra and Mahamudra. They are afraid of falling into the mara realms and losing all of their accomplishments due to the lack of timely guidance from the guru, during the Supreme Bliss state. Because additional detailed instructions are required from the vajra guru, owning a copy of the Highest Yoga Tantra and Mahamudra book still does not entitle you to practice Mahamudra. Please remember this point, and remember it well!

Perhaps someone might say, "Why have you disclosed the Highest Yoga Tantra and Mahamudra, yet you discourage people to practice the teachings? Aren't you being contradictory?"

My reply is that it is my wish that people know about this rare-to-encounter, supreme dharma. If the affinity is not ripe, people will toss away the book. If the affinity is mature, please quickly seek a true vajra guru and ask for transmission. The reason that I write this book is to preserve the teachings in this world. Someone who receives the genuine transmission and pith instructions from a guru may engage in practice, and he or she will gain phenomenal results in their spiritual realization. On the other hand, if an individual practices Mahamudra superficially, without proper transmission from a vajra master, then he or she is likely to fall into the mara states. So, watch out!

My American disciples have wanted to translate *Highest Yoga Tantra and Mahamudra* into English, in order to preserve the secrets and pith instructions in the West forever. I have foreseen into the future that a competent individual will incarnate in the West. Upon encountering this book, he or she will help to spread these teachings so that they will flourish and blossom. This is the main reason that I wrote this book.

In the Supreme Bliss state, the most challenging test is none other than the temptation of sexual desire. The seed of sexual desire is inborn, derived from the genes of our parents. An adept without strong stability is an easy prey to sexual desire. As the psychic heat warms up, an adept will see the beautiful woman that he desires gradually appear in an illusion. Being enticed by her seductive gestures and provocative dances from her naked figure, the adept totally fails the sexual test. Practitioners who do not give into sexual temptations are truly rare. When a practitioner succumbs to sexual desire, he is doomed.

A female practitioner will see an attractive man appearing in her mind. He will tempt her into sexual union. After being persuaded, she will be consumed by sexual pleasure. Thus, the result is the same and she will fall into the hands of mara.

Some overestimate their will power, taking no precautions for sexual temptation. That is because they have not encountered such a vicious challenge. Confucius described men and women on earth as "men and women of food and drink." He also added that "food and sex are part of human nature." There is truth in the sage's statement. I feel that no one can defy sexual temptation, except for a few adepts who have acquired strong capabilities in stillness and stability.

If a practitioner holds any slightest fear, that fear will magnify into a monster born from his own fear during the supreme stage. The single-horned fearsome monster stands several stories tall, glaring at the practitioner, with its eyes as big as the size of bronze bells. It roars and extends his huge tongue, showing its razor-sharp, knife-like teeth. Sometimes a single mara appears, and at times a legion of maras numbering in the tens of thousands come to terrify the practitioner, hindering him from entering into meditative absorption. Even after he enters meditation, the maras still do not give up on distracting him. Eventually, he can no longer eat and sleep properly. His mind simply breaks down. There are many situations where adepts fall into the mara realms due to their fears. Such occurrences are numerous indeed.

During the illusory visions, many events of joy and sadness manifest themselves. For example, one may witness the death of loved ones or see them tormented in hell. One may see one's spouse leave one or run to embrace another person, and so forth. These are examples of sad visions. On the other hand, joyful occurrences are also just as plentiful, and they include visions of seeing oneself as a king, as Sakyamuni Buddha, as the richest man on earth, or one may be approached from the person that one is most fond of.

There was once a Tantric guru who saw a vision of his death during deep meditation. He saw two strings of red pearls hanging from his nostrils, and five arches of rainbows appearing in the sky. His corpse emitted rays of red and yellow lights, and all of his bones displayed multiple colors. His heart remained intact and undestroyed, turning into relics (sariras). He left huge amounts of other relics, around five to six hundred of them, which could fill a big sack. He also saw his disciples cheering at the sight of his many relics. They were all elated.

After this experience, the guru longed to see the entire illusory scene again whenever he entered into meditation because this vision filled him with a great sense of pride. When this desire arose, he found himself experiencing the vision of his own cremation during each meditation session. Finally, when he sensed that something was wrong, it was already too late to erase the illusion. It was pitiful.

On another account, there was an adept who studied Vajrayana from a disciple of the famous Master Atisha. His master had studied dharma at the Tholing Monastery, and he had achieved union with his own inner mandala. He also learned the Three Cycles on Relaxation of the Great Perfection [Dzogpa Chenpo Gyuma Ngalso] and the Profound Quintessence of the Great Perfection [Dzogs Pa Chen Po Klong Chen Snying Thig]. One time, he encountered the following vision during deep meditative absorption:

"Who are you, pretty woman?" the adept asked.

"I am a Tibetan Princess."

"Why are you here?" the adept asked.

"I am here to continue our past affinity." The beautiful lady pointed to another dimension as she spoke.

A vision appeared in another dimension, in which he saw himself incarnating as a senior lama from the Nyingma School. He had practiced the consort practice with the Tibetan princess. Their practice began from the initial level reaching to the deep level, proceeding from the wonderful stage to the mystical stage. He lost his righteous thoughts of enlightenment and was overtaken by lust. His defiled thoughts blocked him from seeing through the illusion of the beautiful woman, who was none other than a pile of skeletons. Being caught off guard, he was led astray into a sexual fantasy. Ever since then, he was unable to pull himself out of it.

Every time the adept entered meditation, he saw the beautiful woman and they were sexually intimate. Initially, he felt that there was nothing wrong with that. However, it was only much later that he realized the vision was a camouflage of the three poisons, five dusts, and six robberies. The adept had lost the aura of light rewarded from the Great Perfection. All his radiance had been transformed into discriminating thoughts of love and disdain. When the beautiful woman failed to arrive, he was afflicted to an extreme. Subsequently, the adept could no longer cultivate, and his proper thought in enlightenment and endeavors in cultivation had become futile. He was worse than a mundane mortal. What a pity!

Here is a verse that I wrote in regards to this incident:

> The practice of union is a supreme path,
> Absence of grasping is the pith teaching,
> Illusion and reality have no difference in truth,
> A smiling beauty is also a laughing skeleton.

There was another adept who studied the Vajrayana teachings with a lay Buddhist known as Daxin. He professed to hold the lineage transmission of Mahamudra from Guru Tilopa and Guru Naropa. He had also obtained the quintessence from Guru Gampopa, and learned the Heart Essence of the Most Supreme Light of the Nine Vehicles. He completed a two-year dark retreat and was very proud of his supernatural powers.

Once, while abiding in the state of profound meditation, he saw himself transforming into a being that was endowed with the thirty-two glorious marks of a buddha. In his vision, he was seated on a white lotus, expounding the dharma to sentient beings. His left hand held the corner of his dharma robe, while his right thumb and ring finger joined together to form a mudra. He gasped at finding out that he was the Buddha!

There are thirty-two major characteristics of a Buddha described in the *Yogacarabhumi Sastra*, which are:

1) feet with level sole; 2) thousand-spoked wheel on the soles of the feet; 3) long, slender fingers; 4) flexible hands and feet; 5) finely webbed fingers and toes; 6) full-sized heels; 7) high ankles; 8) thick calf muscles like an antelope; 9) hands that extend below the knees; 10) well-retracted and concealed male organ; 11) stretchy arms that are equal in length; 12) dark colored hair roots; 13) graceful and curly body hair; 14) golden-hued body; 15) ten-foot aura all around; 16) soft, smooth skin; 17) well-rounded soles, palms, shoulders, and crown at the head; 18) armpits with no hollow areas; 19) lion-shaped body; 20) erect and upright body; 21) full, round shoulders; 22) forty teeth; 23) white and even teeth without gaps; 24) four pure white canine teeth; 25) full cheeks like a lion; 26) saliva that improves the taste of all food; 27) long and broad tongue; 28) deep and resonant voice; 29) bluish-black eyes; 30) eyelashes of a royal bull; 31) cotton-wool soft wisp

of hair between the eyebrows; and 32) fleshy protuberance on the crown of the head.

In the two main Vajrayana mandalas, Sakyamuni Buddha is revered as the main deity in the Garbhadhatu Mandala, and he is aligned with Amoghasiddhi Buddha in the Vajradhatu Mandala. Because Sakyamuni Buddha attained enlightenment in samsara, buddhists in general regard him to be the founder of Buddhism in samsara. [Upon seeing this vision], the Vajrayana adept who was a student of the lay Buddhist Daxin, was immediately filled with joy. Someone even witnessed brilliant lights emitting from his crown, which validated his spiritual attainment as a Tibetan tulku.

After receiving the verification, the adept was confident that he was the reincarnation of Sakyamuni Buddha. He wanted to see the vision of his past dharma reincarnation each meditation session. In his vision, he also saw Bhargava, Arada Kalama, Ksantyrsi and Utpala [teachers of Sakyamuni Buddha] during the time of Sakyamuni, and he discussed and exchanged practice methods with them.

During his meditation, he also felt that he had expounded the dharma for forty-nine years just as Sakyamuni Buddha did. By the time that a guru noticed the adept's odd complexion, the adept was already deeply attached to feeling superior. He had fallen prey to the mara realms. This was indeed a terrible scene. Even at his death bed, the adept still strongly believed that he was Sakyamuni Buddha when, in fact, he was kept in a mental hospital for seven years due to his delusion.

Mahamudra teaches practitioners to think like a child that is at an art exhibition during this spiritual state. A child adores a painting in great detail, looking at one painting after another. However, he or she does not know what the painting is all about. This means that an illusion is unavoidable but the practitioner who has the heart of a child will not be deluded. Though illusions may come, we can choose to ignore them so that their existence has no significance.

In the state of tranquility and extinction, spontaneous delusions may arise from one's subconscious. These manifestations are the result of past karmic obscurations brought to the forefront by our [defiled] thoughts in the present life. At this time, the adept's heart should remain still, dwelling in a state of immovability. The adept should not be affected by any emotional or physical interferences, and he should not attach to any illusions. Otherwise he will be trapped in the mara realms. This method is the same as a child looking at a painting without the mind of attachment. Yet, this level of realization is still not enlightenment. One has to perfect the proficiency of immovability, acquire the undeluded mind in Mahamudra, and merge into it while not being entrapped by delusion. Only then can this be considered as reaching the spiritual state of enlightenment.

Mahamudra also teaches adepts to observe the duality between right and wrong, and purity and defilement. When the mind is undeluded, one will see one's own self-nature and obtain immovability. The fine observation that one develops will help one to pierce through all illusions. This is the Wisdom of Observation. One dharma is the same as many dharmas, and many dharmas are one dharma. The adept is enlightened.

Thus, an illusion is equated to movement in the mind. The same applies to any observations. A child remains unmoved because his heart abides in the state of tranquility. Thus, movement and tranquility lie within these experiences. When one remains unperturbed, this points to the immovability of the mind and illustrates the undistracted state of the true self-nature. Actually, we are still exposed to illusions and observations [but we are just not affected]. There lies profound teachings within these statements.

When one steps into the realm of true reality, one treats life and death, and nirvana and non-nirvana equally. All worldly knowledge becomes zero, and zero is wisdom itself. The consciousness of words disappears. The condition of the universe exists between non-form and non-material, where form is emptiness and emptiness is form; where the heart teaching is the worldly teaching, and the worldly teaching amounts to the heart teaching. Animals are seen as a branch of plants, and likewise plants are seen as a branch of animals. Here, meat is vegetable, and vegetable is meat. All mixtures can be separated into two and combined as one. All things are the same and no different.

The supreme cosmic consciousness is one's own consciousness, and one's own mind is no different from another's mind. The spectrum of life may display a multitude of permutations, yet in truth all entities are derived from the same source of oneness. For example, someone made the following analogy: There is oil in a lamp and when the light is ignited, heat is produced through the light. When the oil becomes exhausted, the light and heat are exhausted as well. The whole process can be divided into four elements, they can also be united as one.

An unawakened individual will see the light as light, heat as heat, oil as oil, and lamp as lamp. Yet, the awakened being naturally discerns both the separation of four entities, and their union as one. Thus, the supreme cosmic consciousness, oneself, others, good people, bad people, and so forth are seen in innumerable forms when they are separated but when they combined, they form one single entity. This is the great realization that I, the Holy Red Crown Vajra Guru, have gained. I abide in the spiritual state of immovability.

The mind and consciousness, seen in an infinite display of many forms, paint a picture of the universe with both subjects and objects. These forms are nothing except for the projections of the mind and consciousness.

I, Vajra Guru Sheng-yen Lu, have acquired the mind of non-obscuration and the mind of non-action of all phenomena, transcending attachment and abiding in the state of immovability. I have never ceased my efforts in cultivation. My attunement with the Dharma-nature is immovable, unhindered and unconditioned. I see [through the truth of] my life and death. What a great feat in realization!

So far, I have discussed the seven-point posture of Vairocana, Eka-grata Meditation, breath regulation and visualization, practice of psychic heat, light drops and inner fire, stillness of tranquility, state of immovability, non-defiled samadhi, and Wisdom of Observation. I have arrived at the realization that all phenomena are illusory. Good people are illusory, and bad people are illusory. All things are changing and illusory.

Don't presume that what I have said is mystical and beyond comprehension. Don't assume that I am playing the enigmatic Zen game with you. My intent is to inspire you to contemplate and discover the truth. If you are wise, then you should atune to my realization. I am trying to awaken the deluded ones, and lead them to the true spiritual state of immovability.

Dawa. Dawa. Dawa. This word, in Tibetan, refers to the highest state of realization [Dawa means moon].

Dream Yoga serves to achieve the continuity of our sacred purity, so that it may not be disrupted by the dream state.

Sheng-yen Lu

14. Dream Yoga of Mahamudra

Many have studied the subject of dreams, and I once said that "dreams arise from our thoughts." However, when we are dreaming, we are often unaware of our state of being in the dream state. When we live in an environment that is not favorable to us, we will have miserable dreams. Likewise, when we live in the comfort of a supportive environment, we will tend to have sweet dreams. Ordinary folks have simple dreams while others, due to external stimulus, have dreams that express different emotions like happiness, anger, sadness and joy. When humans receive external stimulus and absorb their impacts, the corresponding emotions will be released in dreams.

The dream state is one of the activities of our body and mind, and though it is largely illusory, it nevertheless has its place in existence. Dreams are formed from the arising of thoughts, which is also significant to our cultivation. Based on causes and conditions, a dream comes into existence when the respective conditions arise, which is also a form of karmic causation.

As causes and conditions are the result of hidden karmic forces, when all of the causes and conditions ripen, our dreams will respond with a multitude of infinite dream scenarios. Chaotic dreams can greatly impact our lives and cultivation. Therefore, Mahamudra should be practiced during the day time as well as the night time to both ensure that our dreams remain proper and ensure liberation in our life.

My guru once instructed me, "The dream state is like the phenomenon of cyclic existence, fluctuating up and down like the ocean waves, completely manipulated by the force of the winds. The billowing of waves are like the ever-changing phenomenon. If we do not eradicate all these causes and conditions such as ignorance, likes and so forth, the winds and waves will never calm down."

The Sixteenth Gyalwa Karmapa said, "If ordained monks fail to practice the Dream Yoga, then they have no antidote to counteract dream states. Since all people are subject to dreaming, no one is exempted from having twisted and rampant illusions in dreams, unless they have an antidote. Basically, half of their lifetime is spiritually ill, which is considered to be a grievous condition."

I once said that it is more feasible to discipline our thoughts in the day time as opposed to the night time when our thoughts run free and wild. Many monks who appear holy in the daytime are deluded by topsy-turvy dreams at night, where they turn lustful and lose their vital essence through wet dreams. I am not poking fun at these monks, for this is a real issue. The reason that I keep saying this is to motivate these monks to further themselves spiritually, to reach towards the higher truth instead of dwelling in the ill condition of the dream state where they wet themselves in the middle of the night or find their beds soiled. It does not reflect well on a cultivator.

Dream Yoga deals with dream states through the following three approaches:

The first method concerns the technique of the sleeping posture. When we sleep, we must lie on our right side so that our heart rests on the top. We should not sleep on our left side to avoid pressing the heart against the bed. The sleeping posture should resemble that of a sleeping lion. One can refer to the auspicious sleeping posture of the Buddha when he entered into parinirvana. However, unlike the hand position of the auspicious sleeping posture, we should use the right thumb and right ring finger to press lightly over the vibratory veins of the throat. Next, we should place [any of] the fingers of our left hand lightly in front of our nostrils, without pressing against the nostrils. During sleep, it is best to close our mouth and avoid opening it or drooling. In fact, it is really a major problem to snore with our mouths open. It takes time to become accustomed to this sleeping posture. The body should be curved like a prawn, guarding over one's essence and spirit, while the right hand guards the nerve plexus over the throat and the left hand is placed in front of the nostrils. This serves as a subtle reminder that we should not forget about breath regulation during our sleep.

According to the guidance of my guru, since dreams are greatly affected by the vibration of the throat, the nerve plexus at the throat controls the region of dream reflexes. Thus, repeated practice of this sleeping posture, which is an auspicious position, is the key to guarding one's essence and spirit.

The second method involves praying for the blessing of the guru. Those who study and practice Mahamudra are usually guided by a guru. During the day time, we learn how to deal with the dream state while being vigilant to proper thoughts in our mind. We must recognize that the realm of the dream is illusory and unreal. We must foster strong will power to see through the true reality of dreams. Before entering into sleep, we apply the practice as transmitted by the guru by reciting "Om bo li lan ze li" (7 times) [in Sanskrit: Om Vajranjali]. Then by flicking our fingers to the four corners of the bed, we set a boundary that prevents maras from entering.

Before one goes to sleep, one can silently pray for the blessings of the guru, and visualize one's guru and other lineage holders giving us their blessings. We vow to cultivate, attain Buddhahood and achieve control over our dreams, so that we can remain focused and clear. [In time,] our efforts will spill over into our dream state, helping us to gain self-control. All in all, those who practice this method will develop a sense of vigilance that allows them to be immediately aware when they are being deluded in the dream state and be able to recognize that it is only a dream. They will see that it is not real and see through the illusion.

The third method is concerned with performing a visualization prior to sleeping. When we go to bed, we sleep in the auspicious lion's posture. We should visualize ourselves transforming into our principal deity that rests in a sleeping posture. Next, recite the mantra of our principal deity seven or forty-nine times using the vajra recitation approach. Then, visualize our throat chakra emitting strong red-colored rays. This powerful red light radiates towards the ten directions of the universe, completely shattering all illusory visions and manifestations.

This powerful red light also shines upon our body which glows like an illuminated buddha body. This red light will protect you while you sleep. If the practitioner can keep up with this visualization prior to sleeping, he will eventually master this practice and will no longer be deluded in the dream state. Ultimately, he can preserve his vital essence even in the dream.

Why do we visualize the throat chakra emitting red light for protection? This is because the vital spiritual essence (drops) at the throat chakra is the very power that is manifested during the dream state. Our breathing creates vibrations, which in turn produces dreams. Thus, during our visualization prior to sleeping, we should focus on the nerve plexus in the throat chakra. When we perform a visualization during the waking hours, our attention should focus on the third-eye chakra.

In my earlier works I mentioned a practice involving Amitabha Buddha that one can do when one is ill. An individual visualizes himself in the buddha realm of the Western Paradise of Ultimate Bliss [Sukhavati], and recites the heart mantra of Amitabha Buddha while lying in the auspicious posture. He should maintain his clarity of thought and achieve a level of self control, which in turn will allow him to gain rebirth in the Western Paradise. This is a practice to assist sick people.

Actually, when one is skilled in the visualization method prior to sleep, one may vow to seek rebirth in the Western Paradise of Ultimate Bliss. During one's visualization, the throat chakra is most significant because it is the place of the pure and joyous buddha land of Sukhavati. Prior to one's sleep, one should visualize the red light emitted from the syllable AH [in the throat chakra] transforming into visions of Sukhavati, where every adornment is displayed in clarity. If one can achieve such a detailed visualization, then one is bound to attain great accomplishments in the future, and will certainly gain rebirth in the Pure Land.

Thus, the Dream Yoga is an extension of one's practice after the waking hours. It combines day and night into a single domain, wherein contemplation can be consistently maintained during the day and night. Dream Yoga serves to achieve the continuity of our sacred purity, so that it may not be disrupted by the dream state. Hence, whether it is day or night, there is no room for discursive thoughts to exist, and one can abide in a state of purity. Therefore, a singular state is maintained throughout day and night in which all illusory dreams are eliminated, penetrating into the reality of illusory dreams. In this way, one attains the Truth and gains realization.

I would like to reveal a secret of my practice. Whenever I practice the Dream Yoga, I visualize the presence of Bodhisattva Moonlight [Candraprabha in Sanskrit], also known as the Sacred Moonlight Bodhisattva. I visualize a full moon hanging in the sky, radiating pure untainted light. Its light, endowed with unique cooling properties, shines upon me and protects me while I sleep. It removes all illusory dreams and delusions produced from desires. Bodhisattva Moonlight is depicted as a little child dressed in a yellow robe and seated on a red lotus throne.He holds a closed blossom lotus in his right hand and his left hand holds a lotus flower with small leaves that has a half moon disc above it."

In the Diamond Mandala, Bodhisattva Moonlight is seated in the outer northwest court. In the Womb Mandala, he is stationed in the Manjushri Court. Here are the key instructions regarding visualization in Dream Yoga:

Visualize yourself lying in the lion's sleeping posture, like the Buddha entering into Nirvana.

Visualize yourself lying in the lion's sleeping posture, where the physical body disappears under a cloak of red light.

Visualize yourself lying in the lion's sleeping posture, where no dust can contaminate you.

One literally sleeps in the buddha realm, where one finds one's body expanding in size until it becomes space itself and it is emptied of all things. Because the body is emptiness itself, no dust can possibly land on one's body, for there is no body that any dust can cling to in the first place.

It is the supreme heart essence of Dream Yoga that is being revealed here. It is indeed a divine secret, a secret of the Highest Yoga Tantra.

15. Clear Light Yoga of Mahamudra

I have been secretly reciting a mantra called "Dharani of the Great Protectress who is Universally Radiant, Pure, and Incandescent, and the Invincible King of Mantras." Most people simply call it "Dharani of Mahapratisara." Mahapratisara is the bodhisattva's Sanskrit name and she is also known as the Great Wish-Granting Bodhisattva, who is stationed in the Lotus Division of the Womb Mandala.

Mahapratisara Bodhisattva is rich yellow in color. She has eight arms. Her uppermost left hand holds a lotus with a flaming golden wheel on top. The subsequent left hands [from top to bottom] hold a stack of palm-leaf scriptures, a dharma banner, and a noose. Her uppermost right hand holds a five-pronged vajra, followed by hands holding a trident, a sword, and finally a battle axe.

How did she earn the name of Great Wish-Granting Bodhisattva? This bodhisattva is known to grant the wishes of sentient beings as long as they enshrine her statue, chant her epithet, and recite her mantra. By practicing in this way, all wishes will be fulfilled. Another name for this bodhisattva is Maha-Vidyaraja [Great Lord of Lights], which describes the great luminosity that emanates from her body.

This bodhisattva once taught me a secret that all lights are differentiated by varying degrees. This corresponds with what I have said in the past:

The Tathagata Amoghasiddhi radiates magnificent green light born from absolute purity, while the realm of asuras emits a dark, greenish, and ghostly light. There is a world of difference between the two.

The Tathagata Amitabha radiates magnificent red lights born from absolute purity, while the ghosts in the hungry ghosts realm emit weak rays of red light. There is a world of difference between the two.

The Tathagata Ratnasambhava radiates magnificent yellow lights born from wonderful and pure wisdom, while the ghosts in the human realm emit weak yellow and bluish lights. There is a world of difference between the two.

The Tathagata Aksobhya radiates magnificent white lights born from the great mirror-like wisdom, while the ghosts in the hell realm emit hazy and foggy white lights. There is a world of difference between the two.

> "Differentiate the lights with your heart. When this kind of light shines on you and gives you a wonderful sense of comfort and lightness, then this is the buddhas' light. However, when the light is unclear and messy, causing discomfort and disturbance, then you should know that this light comes from the ghostly beings. Moreover, the buddhas' light always shines like a jewel with a luminous flame, that also has the brilliance of a real diamond. The light of the ghostly beings tends to be weak, tempting, and entangling, just like a fake diamond. One must discern these lights carefully to avoid entering into the wrong light and stepping into the wrong spiritual realm."

According to Mahapratisara Bodhisattva's guidance, when one enters the deepest level of meditative absorption, beams of lights will emerge. These lights are the result of the union of absorption and wisdom. The brilliance of the wisdom lights will grow progressively brighter and eventually the lights will illuminate away all ignorance.

Once ignorance is gone, there will be no more hindrances.

When the lights become absolutely clear and transparent, and the adept is able to maintain a stable condition, the adept's lights will merge with the compassionate buddhas' light that encompasses the Dharmakaya Tathagatas of the ten directions. It is like the lights of two mirrors that reflect off one another. The lights from the adept's heart interact and interconnect with the buddhas' light in such a subtle and intimate way that no outsider can possibly perceive or understand it. The union of these two forms of light is supremely pure and sublime, and when one abides in this state of union, this constitutes the Clear Light Yoga.

I once wrote a book recounting this Clear Light Yoga, which became The Illuminated Way of Meditation. It described the following points:

1. Focusing the spirit, wherein one is absorbed with the spiritual eye.
2. Emptying the mind, wherein one sees the true nature of things.
3. Constant quiescence, wherein light appears.

The Clear Light Yoga mainly deals with the doctrine of "merging." In my case, for example, I can merge with pure sunlight when the sun is shining bright, and merge with moonlight during the night. I am able to move in and out of the crown chakra as the light within me projects according to the will of my mind and spirit.

The Tibetan gurus who transmit Mahamudra require that disciples must first recognize the "true nature of lights," and then learn to "differentiate between the grades and degrees of differences between the types of pure lights," before finally recognizing the attainment of the clear light. The first part is theoretical. The second part is concerned with differentiating the differences between the lights attained by the adept. The third part maintains that, through cultivation, the adept's light will obtain responses with the buddhas' light, thereby attaining the realm of wisdom and clear light through the merging of the two lights.

Now I shall reveal a secret to you:

Where does light come from? Light arises from the interval of space between the end of one thought and the arrival of the next thought. Light is produced in this space between thoughts. This is the Mahamudra of Meditative Absorption, the very secret that Noble Tilopa taught: "Think of nothing, and pursue nothing. When you practice no contemplation, no thought, and do think not of the primal consciousness of the universe or the light of the primal self, the clear light shall reveal itself under these conditions. This light does not arise from the primal consciousness of the universe, nor does it come from oneself. It is an inherent pure light that already exists, which reveals itself completely in the space between two connecting thoughts. The light is of itself spiritually clear and vibrant!"

Here's a verse:

The clear and perfect illuminating light is inherent in space.
Between two thoughts the true teaching is found.
With the transmission from the vajra guru,
One merges with the most supreme light.

In the Mahamudra of Meditative Absorption, one who attains the Clear Light Yoga such as the Holy Red Crown Vajra Guru, Sheng-yen Lu, Venerable Lian-sheng, will know that the guru can pierce through all illusory realms and illusory forms with one glance. The authentic buddhas' lights have manifested from my realization. Illusory lights can no longer delude and ensnarl me. The realized one has long attained the joy of liberation, which is true happiness.

The realized individual is thus endowed with pure light; his every act is an expression of a genuine heart that leaves no room for hesitation. He finds all roads to be unhindered and clear. I know that anyone who reaches this spiritual state has arrived at the highest realm of the Mahamudra of Meditative Absorption, which is the ground of Buddhahood. One's body, speech and mind are purified, and all siddhis arising from the fruition of Buddhahood manifest in pure form. This achievement is indeed remarkable.

In principle, either one is active or still, there will be no hindrances. One is free to live among men or live in seclusion until reaching nirvana. Every gesture and action of the realized individual is most dignified, and he is endowed with the greatest of blessings and merits in heaven and on earth. This is the unmatched accomplishment brought about through the Mahamudra of Clear Light.

In the realm of attainment, there exists a very unique truth that I would like to reveal here: "The realm of suchness cannot be experienced through contemplation or observation. It also cannot be described in words. Because the arising and ceasing mind does not exist, no words could possibly provide a complete description of suchness. Righteousness and evil also do not exist. To regard something as being "right" is only the product of the arising and ceasing mind. It cannot be placed in the realm of suchness. This realm of suchness is transcendental. It is beyond explanation and no mortal being can understand it."

It was only after I attained accomplishment with the practice of the Clear Light Yoga that I was able to appreciate what Milarepa had said. Guru Milarepa once told me that any Vajrayana practitioner who gains inner attainment by meditative absorption and whose effort focuses on self-cultivation, will be considered as one who has attained the Buddha-dharma and gained realization.

Anyone whose cultivation does not turn inwardly towards the attainment of meditative absorption, and seeks outer verification instead, is seen as practicing a heretical form of meditative absorption.

Thus, I recognized the following truths:

> The "true path" is to seek enlightenment by turning inwardly. The "heretic path" is to look for enlightenment in the outside world.

Many Buddhist masters, monks, and nuns love to accuse other religions as being heretical. Yet, the difference between the "true path" and "heretic path" is not determined by the religious teachings, but by the separation of "inward focus" and "outward focus." This was my discovery upon gaining realization, and it was indeed the most compelling discovery.

16. Consciousness Transference Yoga of Mahamudra

The Chinese word "li" means to depart, and "she" refers to the physical body. [Consciousness Transference Yoga is called the practice of Lishe in Chinese.] Basically, Lishe refers to the moment when the soul [or consciousness] leaves the physical body. When those who are not involved in any form of cultivation die, they will be led and received by deceased spirits, such as their ancestors' spirits. In such cases, they will end up in the lower spiritual planes.

Some people who have performed virtuous acts will see the gods appearing to receive them, and they will ascend to the heavenly worlds.

Upon death, those who follow the Pure Land School and single-mindedly recite the Buddha's name will experience the Three Sages of the West appearing before them. This indicates that they will gain rebirth in the Western Paradise of Ultimate Bliss, where Amitabha Buddha will appear to receive them.

The four enlightened stages, six mundane worlds, and ten dharma realms embody layers upon layers of truth, which cannot be explained fully in one book. I was almost brought to tears when I was writing the Consciousness Transference Yoga, due to a vision that I had experienced during meditation. Once while meditating in the attic, I saw that only a small number of sentient beings in the universe could ascend to the heavenly realms upon death, and far fewer of them could make it to the Western Paradise. Those who know and practice the Consciousness Transference Yoga are quite rare.

The saha world is evidently filled with many people who do not cultivate. Yet among those who do, many have gone astray, falling into the wrong paths. They have been fooled by spiritual con artists. There are indeed many pseudo dharma masters, fathers, priests, psychic mediums, magicians, masters, and gurus. These individuals appear to be practicing virtuous deeds, but these acts are only disguises. These individuals profit from the donations of the kind-hearted by embezzling more than the amount used for printing meritorious books and performing good deeds.

Among those who end up in the lower spiritual realms and even in hell include these dharma masters, fathers, priests, mediums, magicians, masters, and gurus. Those who do not know any dharma, yet claim to be dharma masters, suffer a greater retribution than the others. When I observed this situation through my meditation, it naturally brought me to tears. I have great pity for sentient beings who do not hear and learn the dharma, and do not know how to cultivate. Therefore I began writing about the simpler methods, and then advanced progressively to this highest teaching of Mahamudra.

I tolerated the slanders that have been aimed at me by these dharma masters, fathers, priests, mediums, magicians, masters, and gurus. I have endured accusations from people, ignoring the vicious verbal attacks from hypocrites. What have I endured all of this for? It is because I need to transfer these special teachings to those who have the right affinity. In this world, only a handful of people know about the Consciousness Transference Yoga, and only few of them would exert continuous effort to spread the supreme Vajrayana teaching. Thus, this act is an expression of great compassion, great guidance, and great sympathy.

Sometimes I worry that the pseudo masters might not appreciate this Highest Yoga Tantra and Mahamudra book. Furthermore, what if they use my teachings to deceive more people? Wouldn't that make things worse? However, this is the way that I am. I feel that all sentient beings should come into contact with the power of the buddhas, experience the dharma taste, cultivate the right teaching, and attain nirvana together. I am thus determined to reveal this material. This is the type of person that I am. I am a straight-forward and unselfish character.

When a person is near death, many illusory visions might emerge. This phenomenon is brought on by the disintegration of the four elements of earth, wind, fire, and water. Eventually, the "physical light" will be extinguished beyond the realm of the six consciousnesses. The physical body and the mind will gradually lose their connectivity, and then the water element will begin to dissipate wherein the mouth and nose will experience dryness. Next the fire element will dissipate, and the body will gradually become colder. After that, the breath or wind will evaporate.

The following is the order of disintegration: First the earth element disintegrates, followed by the water element, the fire element, and finally the wind element. This is the disintegration of the four elements.

Upon the death of the physical body, a person who does not cultivate is led by the forces of their negative karma. This is due to the fact that the person lacks or has a weak inner spiritual essence. He will be led down the path of suffering and be reborn in the six realms, which are: heaven, human realm, asura realm, hell, hungry ghost realm, and animal realm.

However, despite the fact that the physical body and breathing ceases, a cultivated person or adept can still rely on his spiritual essence that he has been cultivating for years. He will see the appearance of smoke and fog, wherein light will manifest. In order to produce light from this smoky fog, he must first purify the three poisons of greed, anger, and ignorance. One should regularly practice purification, so at the departing moment one is able to completely dust off the smallest residual of the three poisons. These three poisons can be further categorized into the thirty-two states of anger, the forty types of greed, and the seven kinds of ignorance. Most importantly, one should completely cut off all strands of attachments, affinities, greed, anger, and ignorance. This is indeed the greatest heart essence.

The first light to manifest typically resembles the glow of a firefly. This is one's own light, which later transforms into a light that is like the light of a lamp. At this stage, when all outer karmic conditions are severed, a massive light will gradually emerge amidst the backdrop of a cloudless sky. The very light that emits from the spiritual essence of the cultivator will ascend and spiral through the central channel, move out of the crown chakra, and join with the light of the great sun.

The Karmapa once told me this:

One's own pure dharmakaya is the "child light."

The nature of the supreme cosmic consciousness is the "mother light."

Here's a verse:

As the physical light forms and fades away,
And thoughts and consciousness are removed,
The consciousness, when eliminated, arises again.
At this moment the clear light begins to dawn.
Light and early dawn blend as one.
Here exists the manifested and unmanifested knowledge,
Merging the manifested into the original ground.
Thus one is said to attain fruition and gain accomplishment.

The above poem summarizes the gist of Consciousness Transference Yoga. At the time of death, a dying practitioner must renounce all worldly karmic affinities such as wealth (thoughts of greed), family ties (thoughts of ignorance), and all love and hatred (thoughts of anger), and cut all karmic ties in the physical world. It is only when all discursive thoughts are eliminated, can one then abide in the realm of the light where the child light manifests itself. It is the very pure state of the child light that attracts the mother light of the supreme cosmic consciousness. As the child light spins and ascends through the central channel, both of these lights merge into one. These two lights are inherently the same, and like old friends who meet again, these pure lights merge with each other. This is, in essence, the final return to the Ocean of Vairocana. This is entering into nirvana and achieving enlightenment.

An individual who has not done any cultivation will experience fear upon dying. This is because he will feel that his body is crumbling like a mountain and he will no longer be able to get up. He will feel an earthquake trembling all around him, and people running in from all directions to kill him. Even though the individual wants to escape from his killers, he will not be able to find his way out. He will experience strong winds, thunder, and lightning. As he runs frantically, he might encounter soft white light, which is the heavenly realm. If he sees and runs into foggy light, then he will enter the hell realm. If he enters a soft yellow light, then he will enter the human realm. If he enters a soft red light, then he will enter the hungry ghost realm. If he enters a soft green light, then he will enter into the asura realm. This is the reality of the six realms of samsara. This is what separates a practitioner from a non-practitioner.

Many readers often ask me if hell really exists. This is my reply, "Hell exists on earth, and many of these hells have already manifested in the human world, such as the operating rooms in hospitals where the hells of opening the skull, grafting the skin, and operating on the heart exist. And in war-torn areas, you will find the hells of knife mountain and fire mountain."

Hell is described in Tantric Buddhism in this way: "In the hell realm there is a huge city with high walls made of black gold. An iron gate opens at each of the four directions of the city, and trees are planted on the sides of the gates, which are hung with banners. A human head is positioned on top of each tree. Lord Yama is in charge, with his left attendant recording bad deeds and right attendant recording good deeds."

This Tantric hell is recorded in the Sutra of Ten Kings. Actually, Lord Yama is known as the Illumination God in Vajrayana. He died and went to the netherworld where he governs the hell realm. The Tantric teachings regard him as a heavenly deity known as Yama Deva, who resides at the gate on the west side of the vajra division in the Womb Mandala. In the Diamond Mandala, he is stationed to the north of the outer court among the Twenty Deities.

In the Tantric depiction of Lord Yama, he is represented as riding on a buffalo. His right hand holds a banner made from human heads and his left palm faces upwards. He has two female devas as his attendants, and two ghostly guards beside him who are dressed in red and black. The guards carry a knife and a battle halberd respectively. Lord Yama rides on a buffalo with his right leg dangling." This image is different from the Taoist depiction of Lord Yama.

Based on my knowledge, the Womb and Diamond Mandalas of Tantric Buddhism are arranged in the order of the star constellations in the cosmos. The heaven and hell realms depicted within Taoism are based on legends, and the hell realm lies beneath the ocean floor. Regardless of the case, I know that the divisions of heaven and hell exist within the human body. When your heart is inclined towards hell, hell will appear before you. When your heart is inclined towards heaven, then heaven will appear before you. Thus, heaven and hell are created by our hearts.

The Consciousness Transference Yoga is a vital quintessential teaching. If one chooses not to believe it, then one will see that what I have said is true when one's time of death arrives.

Those who receive this teaching may use it to deliver their loved ones and other spirits. The merits of this deliverance practice are most supreme.

Sheng-yen Lu

17. Bardo Yoga of Ksitigarbha Bodhisattva

This article discusses one of the genuine bardo practices taught in True Buddha School. The practice was transmitted by the Holy Red Crown Vajra Guru, Venerable Lian-sheng. The article was edited by Lianjing and transcribed by Lianhan, who are two of my disciples in Hong Kong.

The merits of the Bardo Yoga are most inconceivable.

The Bardo Yoga of Ksitigarbha Bodhisattva is as follows:

The participant must adopt a vegetarian for meal at least one day, be bathed and clean, and wear a clean dharma robe before entering the shrine.

Preparation: Set up a sacred alter for Ksitigarbha Bodhisattva, enshrine a statue of Ksitigarbha Bodhisattva, prepare an incense burner, a vajra bell, a vajra scepter, a vajra lasso, ritual implements, a nectar vase, and the five or eight offerings.

Enlist the names of the deceased on tablets, and render offerings of fruit to them. Also offer nectar [water] and [visualize it multiplying] into boundless amounts of spiritual food to the ghosts and gods.

Summon the spirits for deliverance to the shrine with the Ksitigarbha Decree.

(One may burn the Ksitigarbha or rebirth paper money for them.)

1. Perform the Great Homage, the Fourfold Refuge, and the Mandala Offering.

2. Recite the Armor Protection Mantra "Om bo ru lan ze lee" [transliteration; in Sanskrit: Om Vajranjali] seven times. Form the Vajra Mudra and touch the head, throat, heart, left shoulder, and right shoulder. Visualize the vajra protectors guarding you.

3. Invoke the presence of Ksitigarbha Bodhisattva by visualizing him descending to the shrine. Recite the Ksitigarbha Mantra 108 times, "Om ha-ha-ha wei san-mo-yeh soha." Form the root mudra of Ksitigarbha by clasping both hands inwards and straightening the middle fingers so that they are not touching. This is the root mudra of the Ksitigarbha Court. Visualize Ksitigarbha sitting atop your crown and radiating light.

4. Visualize Ksitigarbha transforming into a dot of light, entering through your crown chakra, and then resting on the lotus of your heart. You become one with Ksitigarbha and then enter deeply into the deity's samadhi. After becoming one with Ksitigarbha, you emit lights and may begin the ritual.

5. Recite the Mantra of Opening the Hell 7 times "Om jia-lo-di-ye soha."

6. Summon the spirits to enter into the spiritual realm of the tablets by first reciting their earthly names and addresses,

and then reciting the Vast Summoning Mantra "Namo bu-bu-di-li jia-li-duo-li da-duo-duo-ye." We can also use the vajra bell to empower the spirits, leading them away from darkness, the sea of fire, the netherworld and hell, so that they are able to come to the shrine, and receive the offerings and spiritual food. If the spirits are filled with enmity, we can help them by reciting the Mantra of Enmity Relief, "Om san-tuo-luo jia-tuo soha," while forming the Enmity Relief Mudra.

7. Recite the Repentance Verse for the sake of all spirits:

All past negative karma and hindrances,
Caused by greed, anger, and ignorance from time immemorial,
Committing wrongdoings through body, speech and mind without heed,
Has resulted in the ten sins and five heinous sins.
Breaching countless samaya pledges,
And committing other transgressions endlessly,
I now regretfully and sincerely repent for all of them.
I ask for the buddhas' compassion and forgiveness,
that they may never forsake me until I can attain buddhahood.
(Recite the Repentance Verse 3 times)

Recite the Repentance Mantra: "Om be-dza sa-ma-ya so-de-ah" (3 times).

8. Recite the Ksitigarbha Mantra that Removes Fixed Karma for 3 full rotations of the mala beads [3 x 108 times]. The mantra is: Om pun-lah-mo lin-toh-lin soha. [translitera-

tion; in Sanskrit: Om Pramardani Svaha].

- During the first rotation of the mala, visualize yourself as Ksitigarbha holding a mani pearl. Then, visualize the pearl of light radiating light upon all the spirits. This light pacifies their grievances and animosity, and they are released from their shackles and purified from defilements.
- During the second rotation of the mala, visualize the pearl of light radiating light upon all spirits, which delivers them from the suffering of the three evil paths.
- During the third rotation of the mala, visualize the pearl of light radiating light upon all the spirits, which allows them to gain rebirth at will.
- Sprinkle the nectar to purify their spiritual bodies and empower them with blessings with the sound of the vajra bell, which leads them to liberation.

9. Recite the Opening Throat Mantra 7 times: "Om bu-bu-di-li jia-duo-li da-duo-duo-ye."
   Recite the Ocean of Milk Mantra 7 times: "Namo san-ma-do mo-do-nam om wan."
   Recite the Offering Food Mantra 7 times: "Om mu-li-ling soha."
   Perform the offering of nectar and spiritual food.

10. Recite the respective names of the four Tathagatas seven times, and visualize the four Tathagatas radiating light upon the spirits.
    - *Namo Prabhutaratna Tathagata [the Abundant Treasures Buddha], who is able to break the greed of the hungry ghosts, so that they may receive perfect blessings and merits.*

- *Namo Surupakaya Tathagata [the Dignified Body Buddha], who is able to remove the disfigured form of the hungry ghosts, so that they may have wholesome features and forms.*
- *Namo Vipulakaya Tathagata [the Vast Encompassing Body Buddha], who is able to enlarge the throats of the hungry ghosts, so that they may consume the food being offered.*
- *Namo Abhayankara Tathagata [the Freed-from-Fear Buddha], who is able to pacify the fears of the hungry ghosts, so that they may leave the realm of ghosts.*

11. Perform the Bardo Yoga. Visualize all of the spirits being fully liberated, and released by the light and mudra of Ksitigarbha Bodhisattva. Visualize their spiritual bodies being filled with light, riding on lotus flowers, and ascending to the pure land through the bodhisattva's guiding light. Empower them with the sound of the vajra bell, and offer the nectar and spiritual food again.

12. Recite the Deliverance Mantra 108 times. Visualize the appearance of the Western Paradise of Ultimate Bliss emitting extraordinary brilliance, which shines upon the spirits. The sound of the mantra manifests countless lotuses. Amitabha Buddha radiates great light, and the lotus that he holds in his hand also transforms into countless lotuses, each emitting brilliant light. As the spirits receive the lotuses, their spiritual bodies become bright and liberated.

Recite the Hundred Syllable Mantra 3 times.
Om, be-dza, sah-do sa-ma-ya, ma-nu bah-la-ya, be-dza sah-do deh-nu-pah-deh-cha, zhe-jo mi-bah-wa, soo-do

*ka-yu mi-bah-wa, soo-poo ka-yu mi-bah-wa, an-nu-la-do
mi-bah-wa, sa-er-wa, sid-di, mi-bu-la-ya-cha, sa-er-wa,
ka-er-ma, soo-cha-mi, ji-ta-moo, see-li-yam, gu-ru hum,
ha-ha-ha-ha-hoh, bah-ga-wan, sa-er-wa, da-ta-ga-ta, be-
dza, ma-mee mun-cha, be-dzi-ba-wa, ma-ha sa-ma-ya,
sah-do-ah, hum, pei.*

13. Recite the Verse of Dedication:
    *I now dedicate the merits and infinite blessings of bardo de-
    liverance to all the lost and fallen souls that are suffering.
    May they quickly be delivered to the buddha realm of infi-
    nite light.
    The buddhas of the ten directions and three times,
    Manjusri, Samantabhadra, Avalokitesvara,
    All Bodhisattvas and Mahasattvas,
    Mahaprajnaparamita.*
    Recite the Mantra of Bodhicitta: "Om bo-di-zhi-da ban-
    zha sa-ma-ya ah hum."

14. Perform the Great Homage and exit the shrine.
    Sprinkle the nectar and offer the spiritual food. Burn all
    of the spiritual tablets, the gold and silver nuggets made
    from folded paper, the Ksitigarbha paper money, and re-
    birth paper money.
    This completes the dharma ceremony. May everything be
    auspicious.

Note: This practice is the Sadhana of Ksitigarbha Bardo Yoga. If
you wish to include the Mahayana sutras in this practice, you can
also choose to recite the *Amitabha Sutra* or the *Sutra of the Original
Vows of Ksitigarbha*. The length of recitation depends on the available time of the dharma ceremony. In Vajrayana practices, we focus

mainly on performing clear and precise visualizations. During each dharma ceremony, the Holy Red Crown Vajra Guru Sheng-yen Lu, Venerable Lian-sheng emits the buddha's light. Many participants have witnessed the presence of their deceased loved ones, and some of them have been able to communicate with them. This is the power of Mahamudra. The evidence is so convincing that some Americans with PhDs decided to take refuge in me. The dharma of Tibetan Buddhism has now spread overseas and this is the age where Buddhism is propagated in the West.

Ksitigarbha, the Sanskrit name of Earth Treasury Bodhisattva, is the principal deity of Guru Lian-sheng. The *Sutra of the Ten Wheels of Ksitigarbha* describes Ksitigarbha's many manifestations, such as the forms of Brahma, Mahesvara, Buddha, and Sravaka. All of his manifestations in the six realms of cyclic existence have different names. He resides in the Ksitigarbha Court in the Womb Mandala. In the Diamond Mandala he takes the form of Vajraketu Bodhisattva, who is part of the retinue of Ratnasambhava Buddha.

Ksitigarbha is depicted in many forms. He is commonly seen wearing a five-buddha crown with a luminous mani pearl in his hand, dressed in a kasaya or monk's robe, and seated on a lotus throne. He is often seen holding a staff in one hand. He is most popular in Japan, and statues of Ksitigarbha [Jizo in Japanese] with a shaven head in a standing position are often seen along the rural roads. His other epithets include Jizo Bosatsu, Jichi Bosatsu, Ruciraketu Bodhisatttva, and the Limitless Heart Bodhisattva.

The Bardo Yoga of Ksitigarbha [given above] was originally transmitted to Vajra Guru Lian-sheng by Ksitigarbha himself. Vajra Guru Lian-sheng then transmitted this method to his disciples. This practice text was transcribed by Lianhan and edited by Lianjing, who are my disciples from Hong Kong. Those who receive this teaching may use it to deliver their loved ones and other spirits. The merits of this deliverance practice are most supreme.

Whoever reads this chapter and follows the guidance of one's guru by cultivating the drops and opening the crown, shall attain inner realization of the heart.

Sheng-yen Lu

18. Phowa Yoga of Mahamudra

Miss You Suqing, a disciple of mine who lives in Kumamoto, Japan, asked me about the Phowa Yoga. I replied that the Phowa Yoga is the practice of opening the crown chakra. Accomplishment in this yoga involves the transference of one's consciousness to the dharmakaya [truth body], sambhobakaya [bliss body], or nirmanakaya [emanation body] bodies.

Here is a further elucidation on this yoga:

1. Vajrayana practitioners revere the Phowa Yoga as the most effective, quickest, and most direct method to unblock the crown chakra. Once the crown is opened, one will certainly attain accomplishment and rebirth in the pure land.

2. The attainment of any dharma hinges on the foundations of individuals. Some may cultivate the opening of the crown and achieve results in one day, while others may have to cultivate for forty-nine days before they accomplish the opening of the crown. The difference is due largely to their respective foundations.

3. The Phowa Yoga is one of the major sadhanas of the Ka-

gyupa sect. Some have said that once the crown is opened, the individual can gain rebirth in the pure land at any time. Certainly, when one gains rebirth, the physical body dies. This results in the shortening of one's life. Thus, those who practice this yoga are short-lived. In order to compensate for this, many adepts try to extend their life span by practicing the Amitayus Longevity Yoga.

However, I feel that if one can master the Phowa Yoga well, then one can be reborn in the pure land. Since life itself is an ocean of suffering, and birth, aging, sickness and death are inevitable, it would not matter whether one has a long life or not. Even happiness is a temporal form of suffering. So, why not just leave it all behind? If the Phowa Yoga can shorten one's life span, then why shouldn't one practice it?

4. According to historical accounts, there were two gurus who were revered for their practice of Phowa. They were Venerable Shenglu [1871-1941] and Venerable Duga. I shall elucidate on the Phowa Yoga as follows:

First, position yourself and sit according to the Seven-Point Posture of Vairocana.

Regulate your breath 21 times according to the procedure detailed in the Psychic Heat Yoga.

Then, recite the Supplication Prayer:
Homage to you, Guru Vajradhara!
Offer your protection, enabling me to gain accomplishment in Phowa!
Homage to you, Guru Tilopa!
Guide me to receive your glorious light,

Where the dharma is pure and supreme!
Homage to you, Guru Marpa and Guru Milarepa!
Radiate your lights upon me through the Mahamudra.
Homage to you, all lineage holders!
Above my crown, you sit on your lotus thrones.
With firm and unrelenting faith.
All gurus dissolve in a sea of clear light.
In the supreme dharma realm where the gurus dwell.
I pray that I may swiftly realize the sublime dharma and attain bodhi.
By practicing Phowa and merging into emptiness,
I peacefully dwell in the true buddha realm.

Next, visualize a blue-colored Vajradhara appearing in the magnificent sambhogakaya [bliss body] form sitting at the foremost top [of the refuge assembly] above your crown. His two arms are positioned in front of his chest, with the right arm crossed over the left, holding a vajra in his right hand and a bell in his left. The refuge assembly of lineage holders, in a descending order, forms a straight line. Each one resides within a circular aura of rainbow lights. At the bottom of the lineage, the Holy Red Crown Vajra Guru, Venerable Lian-sheng, who is the root guru in the human world, is seated. Finally, visualize all lineage holders transforming into rainbow lights. The lights dissolve into one's body, constituting the emanation of Vajradhara.

Visualize your entire body becoming void. The central channel in the middle of your body has a larger circumference on top with a smaller opening at the bottom, thus resembling a trumpet. At the opening above the trumpet, the lineage holders of the past are seated. Your central channel is aligned in a straight line with the central channel of the lineage holders. This means that your central channel is linked to the central channel of Vajradhara.

Visualize a blue seed syllable HUM both at your heart and at the heart of Vajradhara.

Then, exhale and shout out the sound "Xi," while visualizing the syllable HUM within your heart ascending towards the top trumpet opening of your central channel. Shout the sound "Xi" continuously 21 times. Throughout the twenty-first shouts, the syllable HUM finally reaches the top trumpet opening of the central channel.

Finally, exhale and shout out the sound "Ga" while visualizing the syllable HUM descending gradually from the top opening of the central channel. Shout the sound "Ga" continuously 21 times. Throughout the twenty-first shouts, the syllable HUM finally returns to the original place within the heart.

Thus, you shout the sounds "Xi" and "Ga" twenty one times. When you shout, you must stretch your vocal capacity and shout out loud. By using the voice to vibrate the syllable HUM within your heart, this will cause the syllable to ascend and descend.

You should practice the Phowa Yoga once a day. By relying on the power of the two seed syllables, along with the supporting visualization and the Seven-Point Vairocana posture, one will successfully unblock the crown chakra.

At the moment of departure, the Phowa practitioner should

forcefully push the HUM at his heart up through the central channel, to merge with the blue syllable HUM within Vajradhara, so that both HUM syllables are united. In this way, the heart of the practitioner is merged with the heart of the lineage holders, wherein the clear light of one's own heart dissolves into the clear light of the lineage holders. This is the significant attainment of the Phowa Yoga.

One must take note of these key points while practicing the Phowa Yoga:

1. Success with the yoga is derived from the guru's blessing. The Vajra Guru is Vajradhara, who is the essence of all gurus. His heart mantra HUM emanates the five wisdom lights, which originally exists within the vajra nature of all buddhas. Our devotion to the gurus must be respectful and sincere, so that we will be endowed with their blessings in return. We should not attempt to practice this yoga if there is no proper guidance from a guru.

2. Though this yoga may seem simple, it is nevertheless powerful. It was originally practiced to achieve great union with the gurus, and the results from the practice can be proven with concrete evidence. When one achieves yogic response, the prana energy pushes upwards towards the crown, which sometimes forms a protrusion, as seen on the statues of the Buddha. A minor bruise may form, and a few droplets of blood and fluid may flow out from the crown. In the past, if someone had opened their crown chakra, they would insert a stalk of kusha grass in their crown as evidence of the opening.

3. When a person with an opened crown chakra dies, his spiritual essence exits through the crown. The soul of the

individual naturally becomes enlightened as it moves out of the physical body through the crown. It ascends up the thread-like central channel that is linked to the crown. Before death and during one's daily practice, one may visualize the light of the lineage holders dissolving into oneself through the crown. This light fills the body's meridians and chakras with power. One may then transform this strength and power into a body of pure light. During each time when I am absorbed in Mahamudra meditation, the pure light of the lineage holders transforms into my inner infinite and pure light, thus achieving union.

4. The awakened reverends found their self-nature and realization by turning inwards. They truly understand the dharma and they practice diligently. It is pitiful that some reverends don't understand the [true meaning of cultivation], and they are only interested in applying psychic abilities for mundane affairs. Now I only care about meditative absorption that leads to inner realization, and not other non-Buddhist practices. If my disciples truly understand this point, then they can be considered true disciples of True Buddha School. They should also embrace the cultivation of light drops!

I pity the American lifestyle where people indulge in materialism. In their sermons, many priests ask people to worship God, and maintain kind and loving thoughts. In return, God will bless them. Through prayers, the line of communication with God will be opened, and when the time comes, the faithful will ascend to his heavenly kingdom. However, reliance on prayers, as taught within Christianity and Catholicism, is based on the teaching of seeking outside oneself. If the hindrance of ignorance is not removed, then prayers alone cannot help one to reach the heavenly kingdom. Thus, in the end, a large number of believers within Catholicism and Christianity are not saved because they only know how to seek the truth outside themselves, and they do not know how to seek the truth within. Thus, they are trapped at the superficial level and they are unaware of the inner truth.

The Phowa Yoga blends both approaches of seeking outwardly and inwardly into one method, and it seeks a response from the deities. This is the response attained at the dharmakaya [Truth Body] level. Today I have many western disciples who are aware of this practice, and a few of them have achieved the opening of the crown. They feel a sense of tranquility in their body and mind, and abide in the supreme samadhi of stillness.

The Vajrayana teachings have spread to the West, and the practice of Vajrayana is certainly an eye-opening experience for westerners. The practice of Mahamudra has allowed me to become one with the universe, with my guru, and with all sentient beings. Indeed, the true teachings of self-realization have been established in the West and many westerners have taken refuge.

Whoever reads this chapter and follows the guidance of one's guru by cultivating the drops and opening the crown, shall attain inner realization of the heart. Had I not made my compassionate vows to help all sentient beings gain realization of their true mind, it would be impossible to guide the pure light into the hearts of sentient beings, and bring great benefits to them.

To **purify** spirit and mind, we must mitigate crudeness such as fear, doubt, vanity, pride, hatred, slander, selfishness, hypocrisy and so forth. We must transform the crude natures of the spirit into refined natures through the practice of Mahamudra.

Sheng-yen Lu

19. Samadhi of Observation

What exactly is the Samadhi of Observation? It is the partial or total spiritual sensation as experienced by the individual when he is infused with the cosmic spirit during the meditative absorption in Mahamudra.

My friends, I have long attained the above spiritual state. It took many years of endeavor and continual cultivation in America. The journey I am embarking on is the supreme path of joy and happiness. Many worldly reverends and masters condemned me both verbally and in writing. They believe that their actions would petrify Master Sheng-yen Lu, or at least cause him to have insomnia. They are all wrong. I have already united with the supreme consciousness. They thought that they had humiliated me; in fact, they were attacking the Supreme One. I have long gained the mind of no impediment. All forms of verbal attacks and slanders have no effect on me.

I am aware of all practices of inner cultivation, and I cultivate with due diligence daily. I also incorporated my cultivation with the techniques of Mahamudra and breath control. As a result, I have attained a state where I can perform all rituals of Mahamudra with full concentration. I can enter deeply into the samadhi of meditative absorption. My spiritual capacity cannot be conceived of. My undividable intimacy with the Supreme One cannot be moved slightly even by the most divergent power of the maras, which leads people towards crudeness and degradation.

The Supreme One is omnipresent, and humans are originally part of the Supreme One. People should transform their crude nature into a refined state through inner cultivation and meditation. All means of cultivation serve to help us abide by spiritual protocols, and partake in the true path of joy and happiness. Beginning with sincerity and devotion, people will then be uplifted towards inner cultivation and meditation.

Everything in this universe is created and evolved by the spiritual current of creation, and it works in a cycle. One who was once coarse and materialistic must eventually transform and refine their spiritual nature, so that it can merge as one with the primordial consciousness. Such is the law of the cosmic consciousness.

The spiritual state of Mahamudra is the highest spiritual level, in which one is absorbed in a calm-abiding samadhi state of oneness. Such spiritual experience is beyond any form of description, but through the hand of an authentic guru such as the Holy Red Crown Vajra Guru, it may be brought to light. The spiritual master guides people and teaches them how to get rid of darkness and ignorance, and leads his disciples towards the truth. Together, they experience the complete state of true knowing and joy within the spiritual state of Mahamudra.

Some people have suspected that Master Sheng-yen Lu has ulterior motives. But Master Sheng-yen Lu has only one motivation and one mission, which is to ferry people to the other shore. That is my sole purpose: to deliver the human spirits to the pure land, which also corresponds with the natural law of the universe. The greatest gravity of the universe and the ultimate goal of cosmic consciousness, is to bestow perfect liberation to all human beings by dissolving our spirit and mind into the greater non-sectarian world of cosmic consciousness. Thus, my motivation is selfless and detached, and it is a mission of complete sacrific, that I will devote my entire life for.

The physical body is composed of the five elements of earth, water, fire, wind and space. The whole universe is similarly composed of the five elements, including solids, liquids, heat, air and ether. Solid matter is the earth element, liquid is the water element, heat is the fire element, air is the wind element, and ether is the space element.

To purify spirit and mind, we must mitigate crudeness such as fear, doubt, vanity, pride, hatred, slander, selfishness, hypocrisy and so forth. We must transform the crude natures of the spirit into refined natures through the practice of Mahamudra.

The following include the details about the Samadhi of Observation:

1. The forms and features of all things in the universe are primarily "equal." The forms of the highest beings, such as the Buddhas, extending to the lowest living micro-organisms are all born from the same source.

2. All sounds are primarily "equal," from the sounds of the highest mantra extending to the lowest sounds of obscenities. All sounds are born from the same source.

3. All realities of consciousness are primarily "equal." From the highest realized state of consciousness in the universe to the lowest consciousness of micro-organisms, all are born from the same source.

I realized that the past, present and future states are indivisible. One is all and all are one. All phenomena of birth and extinction are caused by the arising of illusions. The ability to make this observation is called the Samadhi of Observation, which can penetrate the true nature of all phenomena.

Thus, the individual spirit originally came from the spirit of the supreme cosmos. The practice of Mahamudra serves to liberate the individual spirit, which is bound by karma and drifts aimlessly in the universe. One must return the spirit back to its original spiritual state of supreme joy and happiness. Through Mahamudra training, the spirit is relieved from karmic burdens and retribution, and it can quickly re-unite with the spirit of the Supreme One. Hence, there exists no difference between the individual spirit and the Supreme Spirit.

What am I? I am a master who guides human beings towards the perfect path of the supreme consciousness. I come from the supreme consciousness. I am now employing all of my strength and means to help humankind understand the knowledge of spirituality. I have arrived at the state of non ego-grasping, and I am no longer enticed by any worldly circumstances. I have long been able to extract myself from the bounds of the material world and have realized the ultimate truth.

My heart is enlightened, and I have attained the Samadhi of Observation.

I am able to observe illusions and see their underlying true reality. I am released from the dream that was fabricated by Lord Brahma. I have achieved this through the practice of Mahamudra.

20. Mahamudra of Permanence, Bliss, True Self, and Purity

One time during deep meditation, I travelled spiritually to Fanyin Cave, which is located at Mount Putuo [in China's Zhejiang Province]. The cave is sandwiched between two steep cliffs. When the sea tumbles into the cave, it responds with thunderous roars. For this reason, the cave is named the Buddhist Sound Cave and it is one of the main attractions at Mount Putuo. In the vicinity of the cave, a temple was constructed.

I once read the book named The Legends of Mount Putuo, which recounts the miraculous experiences that the pilgrims encountered at Mount Putuo or Fanyin Cave. Those who had a strong Buddhist affinity would see the appearance of Guanyin Bodhisattva, Sudhana Nagakanya [naga lady], or the Taiping Bird, which is the attendant of Guanyin. These beings appear according to an individual's past karmic affinity, and everyone sees a different manifestation.

During my deep meditation, I was surprised to find myself arriving at Mount Putuo, so I visited the Fanyin Cave. While I was paying homage, I saw an immortal appearing before me. The immortal was not Guanyin, Sudhana or Nagakanya. This immortal held a horsetail whisk in his left hand and a crossed-vajra staff in his right hand. He wore a jeweled crown and a plain robe.

The celestial being revealed himself, and together we ascended to the clouds.

"Lian-sheng, do you recognize who I am?"

"No, I don't."

"I am Varsi."

"I am sorry, but I really haven't heard of your name. Please enlighten me on our past connection."

Then, the immortal Varsi related this story: He was a fire-worshipping Brahman practitioner in India. Once, he journeyed to Fanyin Cave and he enjoyed the serenity and peace there so much that he decided to stay. He made a straw hut near the cave, and he continued his practice of killing and sacrificing animals through the fire ritual, as offerings to heaven. Subsequently, due to his heavy karma of killing, he had fallen into the hell realm and suffered unbearable torment after his death.

Guanyin Bodhisattva of Mount Putuo visited the hell, and there she saw Varsi in great agony. She learned that Varsi had practiced at the Fanyin Cave before, so Guanyin taught him the Yoga of Permanence, Bliss, True Self, and Purity. Thus, Varsi practiced this yoga with unwavering determination. Gradually, he was able to absorb light and free himself from the hell of extreme heat and cold. From then on, he focused on this yoga and sincerely revered the Triple Jewels. Eventually, he attained the Akasagarbha Body ["Space Womb" Body] and became Guanyin's attendant. This was his past affinity.

"Immortal Varsi, what exactly is the Yoga of Permanence, Bliss, True Self, and Purity?"

"Lian-sheng, what types of things cast off light?"

"Well, I know the sun shines, and so does the moon, the stars, lightning, lamps, fire, candles, and so forth."

"Lian-sheng, do you know how to absorb light?"

"Yes, I can absorb all lights into the spiritual eye."

"That's right. When you absorb light into the spiritual eye, the third eye will open. When you absorb light into the heart, you will develop telepathy. When you contemplate with your heart, which is like a mirror reflecting light, you achieve the supreme wisdom of contemplation," Immortal Varsi said.

"How do we teach this yoga to sentient beings?" I asked.

Immortal Varsi taught me the following method:

Take a round mirror of any size and request your guru to bless it. Hang the mirror in the center of your shrine.

If you stay at home or go out, regardless of the time that you return, you should employ the method of Breathing In and Storing All Energy to suck all the light energy into your heart. This includes the sunlight, moonlight, starlight, firelight, candlelight, and lightning.

When you enter your shrine, you need to release the light from your heart and let it dissolve into the light of the mirror. Through your visualization, every time that you exhale, your breath releases light into the mirror. After each time, the light is captured by the mirror and dissolves into it.

Then, recite the Mantra of Absorbing Sunlight: "Om fu-ri-luo tuo-dou-fan [OM VAJRA DHATU VAM]," also known as the Vairocana Mantra. You may also recite the following mantra for sunlight or the other lights: Om a-mo-ga huai-lu-jia-na ma-ha mu-de-la ma-ni ba-de-ma ji-fa-la bo-la-fan-er-da-ya hum [OM AMOGHA VAIROCA-NA MAHAMUDRA MANI PADMA JVALA PRAVARTAYA HUM].

After you exhale light into the mirror, recite the above mantra once.

You must persevere with your practice until the mirror radiates light. This light is different from the normal light that we usually see. It embodies the magnificent brilliance of the five-colored lights, which represents the "true heart and true mirror." From this time onwards, whenever you start to visualize, you shall find yourself being dissolved completely into the spiritual realm of illumination. This realm is the world of "Permanence, Bliss, True Self, and Purity."

This yoga combines the light from oneself, the mirror, and the heart into one unified light. In this realm, only complete tranquility exists. The realm of the mirror light is neither emptiness nor existence, nor is it non-emptiness or non-existence. Words fail to describe such a spiritual state. It is the state of Permanence, Bliss, True Self, and Purity, created by lights from the desire realm.

"What is special about this spiritual realm?" I asked Immortal Varsi.

"This realm is actually a hidden world. Those who live in this world cannot be harmed by any types of curses or black arts. No spell can come close to them. This spiritual state is said to be an illusory model of nirvana, or a resemblance of the state of nirvana. Hence it is a world of complete tranquility. An adept of this particular yoga will radiate infinite light. However, after one validates this state, one should not be content and abide in this realm forever. One should further progress."

"Why so?"

"Arrival at this spiritual state is merely a selfish accomplishment, wherein one only indulges in living at ease and forgets about sentient beings. The highest level that one can reach is that of an arhat [a self-liberated being]. We don't cultivate Vajrayana and gain realization to only benefit ourselves. Rather, our ultimate goal is to help others and ferry them to the other shore. Thus, the adept of this particular yoga must practice other dharmas to accomplish this important mission."

"Thank you, Immortal Varsi, for your kind instructions." I expressed my gratitude sincerely.

Immortal Varsi disappeared, and I returned to Seattle and came out of my meditation.

The Mahamudra of Permanence, Bliss, True Self, and Purity is indeed a Hinayana practice, with the target of achieving the level of an arhat. No wonder bodhisattvas who are already enlightened and have even reached the level of perfect nirvana, choose not to dwell in the state of stillness. Instead, they aspire to liberate sentient beings and fulfill their vows by returning to samsara and continuing their salvation work. They appear as either a bodhisattva, a great teacher, or a master. Throughout each age, these great bodhisattvas have made vows to deliver all sentient beings, including those who dwell as micro-organisms on earth and those who suffer in the three evil paths, up to the celestial beings in the heavens. All of them are led to the path of enlightenment. The bodhisattvas vow never to enter into Buddhahood, nirvana, nor to abide in tranquility, so long as a single sentient being still suffers.

Hinayana students often stop cultivating when they become enlightened, whereas Mahayana students are taught not to abide in nirvana. Even after one has entered nirvana, one should re-emerge and continue to follow one's vows. It is a continuous mission, and nirvana should not be seen as the end of the path.

Those who practice the Yoga of Permanence, Bliss, True Self, and Purity, must understand that the mind is the source of all spiritual power. However, due to past karmic hindrances, people frantically cling to the material world, without any desire to discover the inner illumination. They are tempted by money and fame, and completely ignore their inner light. Therefore, life after life, they are entrapped in cyclic existence. Today, you have read this book. You have learned about the inner light, and know about the liberation through the Highest Yoga Tantra and Mahamudra. Thus, you are indeed fortunate and blessed with past karmic affinities.

After reading this book, you should seek guidance from a genuine master. Also, you shall know that you are endowed with an abundance of treasures and brilliance. If you practice diligently without being disturbed by mundane matters, then nirvana will be within reach. The Yoga of Permanence, Bliss, True Self, and Purity is simple, and it can be mastered by true adepts.

Here is a verse:

Immortal Varsi has attained nirvana,
Through the light of Permanence, Bliss, True Self, and Purity.
Free from dissonant emotions, in tranquility he dwells,
Yet, he must leave and vow to return later.

21. Mahamudra of Severing Delusion

The essential purpose of learning Mahamudra is to penetrate the true existence of reality. That is why the Mahamudra adept is the wisest person in the world because he or she is neither attached nor deluded. Before reaching the non-deluded state, Vajrayana practitioners are prone to fall into four deviated paths, so we must recognize what these four paths are and commit them to memory.

The first deviated path is the delusion of emptiness. There is a monk who studies the teachings in the Satyasiddhi School and the Three-Treatises School, which are branches of the Sunyata, or School of Emptiness. He sees all things as devoid of intrinsic nature. He also practices meditation and focuses on renouncing self-grasping. He is aware that all dependent originations are inherently empty in nature, and that the egotistical self and its possessions are non-existent. His final spiritual destination will be the Heaven of Boundless Emptiness, the first heaven of the Realm of Formlessness, which is among the Three Realms and the Nine Levels. This monk thought that he had attained enlightenment.

In fact, this monk who is attached to the nature of emptiness can only attain the Realm of Formlessness. Practitioners in this category often engender the heart of never returning to the human realm. They think that they have merged with emptiness and have unlinked themselves from the chain of birth and death. However, all that they have experienced arose from a sense of selfishness, for people who indulge in the nature of emptiness are unable to generate the heart to deliver sentient beings. They actually mislead themselves to a state of "stubborn void." They hold the heterodox view that does not recognize the existence of cause and effect, and they are attached to the views and understanding of emptiness. Such a spiritual level is not comparable to the bodhisattva state that embodies the true reality of Mahamudra. Thus, this is the first wrong path.

When you ask this monk about what truth is, his reply is, "Truth is emptiness." When you ask him about delivering sentient beings, his reply is, "It is empty to deliver sentient beings." What about meditation? His reply is, "Meditation is emptiness." His reply, no matter what you ask, is always "emptiness." He is completely attached to the ideal of emptiness. An individual who practices this form of meditation will attain the Samadhi of Emptiness, whose highest spiritual state is the Heaven of Neither Thought nor Non-Thought. When one is dwelling in this meditation, the highest levels that one can hope to reach are the four spheres of existence in the formless realm.

The second deviated path is the delusion of scriptures. I once said that there are indeed many great scholars and venerables who are completely versed in the study of the sutras and scriptures. Whenever they discuss principles based on the sutras, they deliver them clearly and coherently. If they are approached with questions, they will support their arguments by quoting from the sutras and scriptures. Christians are absorbed with the Bible; Buddhists, the Buddhist Canon; Taoists, the Taoist Canon. I am not trying to discourage you from reading the sutras and scriptures, but I want you to read them, apply them creatively, realize their meanings, and create new insights. I do not encourage the memorization of texts, nor do I want you to become a bookworm and bury yourself in the scriptures.

Being well-versed in the scriptures is useless. To mentally master all sutras and scriptures without actually practicing and generating new insights through the teachings, is nothing more than being a blind follower. These scholars and monks are not able to go beyond the boundaries set by the sutras and scriptures, and are unable to put them to good use. Hence, they become too involved with the scriptures. Such is the condition of attachment to the "mara of words." This condition is a form of delusion, which involves a sense of intellectual complacency that feeds the academics. They believe that by understanding the meanings contained in the scriptures, they have realized the truth. Through this approach, they isolate themselves in their thoughts and no longer pursue the inner true reality of Mahamudra. To be armed with only an intellectual mastery of the scriptures and gaining no progress in one's spiritual level, illustrates the situation of being bewildered by the scriptures and deluded in the mara realm of words.

Whenever you ask any monk who falls in this category what exactly is truth, his reply would likely be, "A certain scripture says it is like this." When you ask him about delivering sentient beings, his reply would be, "Go read the sutras and realize the meaning of the words." Then, if you continue with the question of meditation, his reply would be, "Meditation is exactly what is written in the scriptures."

All that the monks ever know and say when they preach the dharma is quoted from the sutras and scriptures, and they regard the truth written in the sutras and scriptures to be the perfect truth. Actually this is a grave mistake. The Mahamudra of Dispelling Delusion is to be actualized in practice. The scriptures should never be held as the final word, for they are only supplementary to our cultivation. We must regard the inspiration gained from actual practice and actual realization as primary, for the Mahamudra leads to a limitless expansion of ideas and an expansion in cultivation. If we want any yogic response, then we must not be engrossed with the scriptures.

The third wrong path is attachment to the practice of stilling thoughts. When I began teaching the practice of Mahamudra, I encouraged people to still their discursive thoughts. However, when a day comes when you find there is no way to still your thoughts, then you must stop trying. It may seem like a paradox, but it is not. It is really the progression of the following three phases of cultivation:

1. Stilling the mind - First we learn to stop discursive thoughts.
2. Letting the mind be - Let the discursive thoughts run wild.
3. Observing the thoughts - Like standing by a river, watch the flow of thoughts moving like the river water, while one remains unaffected by them.

The Tantric practitioner must cultivate according to these three phases. When you reach a point where you realize that the thoughts cannot be stopped, then stop trying and simply allow the thoughts to flow naturally. This is because the more you try to stop your thoughts, the more that the discursive thoughts will be produced. Therefore, you would be better off to simply let the discursive thoughts continue on their own and see the process as a natural thing. By letting the thoughts flow and subside on their own accord, they will appear to diminish.

If we focus on stopping the arising of discursive thoughts, then it can turn into a kind of obsession with stilling the thoughts. This will have an adverse effect on us if we push too hard to stop them from arising. When the discursive thoughts flow unceasingly, the process of attempting to stop them likewise increases. Eventually, the situation becomes similar to the Yellow River bursting its banks, where all desires and thoughts flood the mind and destroy our efforts of cultivation overnight. Thus, the Tantric practitioner who practices

Mahamudra must understand the three phases of cultivation, where one first stills thoughts, and if the thoughts are unstoppable, then one should let the thoughts run their course. Finally, we transform the discursive thoughts into thoughts of observation. This is the right way to practice.

A monk once told me that when he was cultivating the method of stilling his thoughts, he was unaware of the method of diversion. Whenever a discursive thought arose, he would slap himself once. Eventually his face became swollen, but it did not help to stop his thoughts. Later, he took a needle and pricked himself whenever he had to stop his thoughts. But still, this did not stop his thoughts. Finally he thought of cutting his penis. I told him that even if he cuts off his penis, it would not help to reduce his discursive thoughts. Do you really think that by becoming a eunuch you will not have sexual thoughts? Eunuchs have sexual thoughts more than anyone else. We call this "the bare itch." The only way to deal with discursive thoughts, aside from stopping them, is to first still the mind. When this does not work, then one should switch to the approach of letting one's thoughts run freely. After doing this for some time, switch to the approach of studying the buddhas' statues to appreciate their sanctity, and divert your thoughts in a natural way. By adopting this approach you will not become attached.

It is the wrong path for a Tantric practitioner to become obsessed with the act of stilling the mind.

The fourth wrong path is to be obsessed with performing multiple practices. There are many practices in Vajrayana. A practitioner may prefer one practice over another and become fickle, by adopting different practices at different times. Even his or her choice of principal deity may change all the time, and eventually the individual can't make up his or her mind which principal deity to follow.

Today, I, the Holy Red Crown Vajra Guru, have transmitted many Tantric methods, and those that have yet to be transmitted number in the thousands. If I decide to transmit all of those methods and let the readers learn them, then even a hundred lifetimes would not be sufficient to cultivate them. At the same time, the individual won't be able to gain any spiritual responses. The practitioner only needs to pick the one practice that suits his or her nature the most and stick with that practice. Once the practitioner gains yogic response, it is only natural that he or she will gain responses with other practices. This is a key point.

He who receives the Mahamudra has long realized this truth. All of his or her actions stem from Mahamudra, and they are completely absorbed in the state of Spontaneous or Essence Mahamudra (Sahaja Mahamudra). This is liberation. This form of liberation is called "the dharma is really no dharma." All of these practices can be put aside, for his or her every action in life constitutes "all dharma." The individual abides perpetually in the state of liberation, and his or her expression of "all dharma" is done for the sake of sentient beings. This is the most important attitude held by a realized person. Thus, putting on a shirt is Mahamudra. Relieving oneself in the toilet is Mahamudra. Washing one's hands is Mahamudra. Thus, an obsession with multiple practices is itself a delusion. I just want to remind you not to be obsessed with multiple practices. Remember it well! Remember it well!

22. Levels of Mahamudra

Once, in my meditation, I went on a pilgrimage to Mount Wutai. Mount Wutai is located in the northeast part of Wutai County in Shanxi Province. It is also known as Qingliang Shan, the Cool and Pleasant Mountain. There are four renowned mountains in China, which include Mount Wutai (the Pure Land of Manjushri Bodhisattva), Mount Emei (the Pure Land of Samantabhadra Bodhisattva), Mount Jiuhua (the Pure Land of Ksitigarbha Bodhisattva), and Mount Putuo (the Pure Land of Avalokitesvara Bodhisattva). In an earlier chapter, I mentioned about my trip to Mount Putuo during a deep meditation where I had met the Immortal Varsi.

At Mount Wutai, I saw the cluster of five majestic peaks protruding through the clouds. The mountain is covered with snow throughout the year, so there are no trees or grass on the mountain peaks, except for the formation of five rock platforms. I believe this is how Mount Wutai (which means the five terraces) obtained its name. I saw the Mingyue Pond and Kuanhai Temple, and paid homage at the Longquan Temple.

At the South Platform, I paid homage at the Pishan Temple and Guangji Temple. I found that the land formation of Mount Wutai was simply fantastic, as the platforms in the east, west, south, and north towered above, while the central platform was much lower by comparison. The North Platform is formidable. The whole formation of Mount Wutai looks exactly like a natural lotus blossom. This mountain has bred many legends and amazing stories, such as the appearance of fragrant clouds, shadows of light, aureolas, manifestations of arhats, lotus flowers and so forth. These religious legends are quite inspiring and touching.

Although Mount Wutai is the sacred ground for Chan or Zen Buddhism, many lamas from Mongolia and Tibet were once based there. However, all these things are things of the past.

To make a pilgrimage to Mount Wutai during deep meditation was itself a mark of rare affinity. When I was standing before the Longquan Temple, I was astonished to see the gods of Eight Kumaras [Eight Youths] at play. Naturally, these eight young youths are beyond human vision. I was rather surprised at this sighting, and noted that each youth had three hair knots tied on his head. They wore celestial garments and held different implements in their hands. They stood on lotus flowers and they were chasing each other.

It took me a while to figure out the divine background of the eight youth. When I think of Manjushri, the answer dawned on me right away and I shouted, "They are the Eight Youths of Manjushri!"

Among the retinues of Manjushri Bodhisattva, these eight youths represent the eight wisdoms of Manjushri. They are stationed around the Astadala County, [Eight-petal Court] of the Womb Mandala. These eight youths accompany and surround Manjushri: In the northeast, there is Kesini; in the southeast is Upakesini; in the east is Citrah; in the southwest is Vasumati; in the north is Akarsani; in the south is Jaliniprabha; in the west is Vimalaprabha, and in the northwest is Acintyamati. I shouted loudly and the eight youths suddenly noticed my presence.

Immediately, they flew to my direction. Acintyamati, who held a precious stick, bowed towards me and said, "So it is you, White Pad-makumara from the Maha Twin Lotus Ponds in Sukhavati." The rest of the seven youths were just as surprised and shouted, "It's White Padmakumara! It's White Padmakumara!"

These eight youths, along with myself, added up to nine kumaras or youths. Our gathering was indeed a special and rare occasion. I inquired about their merits of cultivation and this is what they told to me:

> Kesini - Became accomplished through no thought.
> Upakesini - Became accomplished through the merits of generosity.
> Citrah - Became accomplished through constant stability of the body of form.
> Vasumati - Became accomplished through donating to and aiding the poor .
> Akarsani - Became accomplished through the vows of delivering sentient beings.
> Jaliniprabha - Became accomplished through the absorption of light through his great compassion.
> Vimalaprabha - Became accomplished through the pure light of great wisdom.
> Acintyamati- Became accomplished through the purest, most supreme, and all-pervading wisdom.

They asked me, "What brought you here, Padmakumara?"

"As I entered into meditation, I travelled throughout many celestial realms and places. As I am now writing the book *Highest Yoga Tantra and Mahamudra* for the world, I am here to build a bridge of good affinity between heaven and earth," I said.

Then the eight youths revealed to me the following four levels of

Mahamudra:

The first level is "warming." When one ignites the fire within the body, this is "ignition." This spot of fire is seated right at the base of the central channel. Once this fire is ignited, it rises along the central channel and burns through every channel knot. When this fire burns the channel knots in the body, it is as good as burning away the negative karma. The fire burns away the lustful desire, discursive thoughts, and ego-grasping. As each channel knot is burned away, our cultivation power increases proportionately.

At this stage the body feels warm. If the body feels cold, then something has gone wrong. The comfortable warmth corresponds to the spiritual state of ultimate bliss. The rising of the inner fire can assist the practitioner to see the "True Reality of Mahamudra." Whether one gains achievement or not, depends on the rising of this inner fire.

The second level deals with "breaking." When the inner fire ascends to the spiritual eye, it will produce light. If the practitioner's spiritual eye can radiate light, then he has validated and achieved accomplishment in the meditative practice of the spiritual eye. The great luminosity that is obtained can "break" all darkness, at which time the "true reality" is completely revealed within this light of the spiritual eye. Thus one gains the third eye. Subsequently, by "breaking" or "opening" the crown, every phenomenon of the universe is completely revealed before the individual's eyes, and nothing remains hidden from one's sight. This "breaking" is attributed to the progressive "warmth." The "warmth" inevitably leads to "breaking;" without it, nothing happens. When one reaches this second level of "breaking," one arrives at the "Realization of Mahamudra."

The progress of warming to breaking is fostered by one's continuing effort in stability or concentration. Naturally, one will encounter some mara hindrances, so one must clearly recognize the detours or distraction, and one should always remain vigilant in the path of cultivation.

The third level involves "preserving." To preserve is to cultivate with diligence and happiness, without any trait of sluggishness. The practitioner will have to overcome many trials to advance oneself from the "warming" level to the "breaking" level. However, if one aspires to help sentient beings, he must acquire the mastery of tolerance. It is because mara is capable of entering into the hearts of sentient beings and creating many negative situations to disrupt the practitioner. You will be caught in a battle between the mara and the buddha. Many people will slander you. You will even cause the formidable mara to be jealous and sneak into the hearts of secular monks to turn against you. This is the similar case of the monk Xuanzang of the Tang Dynasty. On his mission to bring valuables sutras back from India, all the demons wanted to taste his flesh and eat him alive. At this stage, practitioners should maintain an unhindered mind, abide in the tranquil state, and remain unaffected by outer turmoil. One is said to arrive at the level of preserving, when he can always remain firm and vigorous in the cultivation effort. At that time, his wisdom will brighten and his spiritual conviction will be strengthened as well. This is because the achievement of stability is tempered through perseverance and tolerance.

While abiding in this spiritual state, the practitioners must endure the vicious remarks from common Buddhists and fake Vajrayana masters. However, we must continue to practice the supreme dharma with the attitude of perseverance and with the concentrated mind. Only then can we progress onto the wonderful path of Mahayana and receive the true heart seal. Only then can we truly abide in the state of self-nature.

The fourth level is "validating." Having validated the supreme dharma, the practitioner's light is merged with that of the supreme consciousness. This is the state of nirvana. However, what the practitioner really wants to attain is to transform the "supreme bliss of tranquillity of nirvana" into the "supreme dharma bliss of bodhi." One is no longer bounded to cyclic existence and one observes all things with one's wisdom eye. Although one has all sorts of entanglements, one still lives in the trouble-free light of absolute realization. This is indeed an extraordinary state of realization.

The individual who has validated the fourth level also realizes that the truth of bodhi is beyond words. All phenomena are empty in nature within the dharma realm, and the empty dharma nature is essentially the bodhi itself. There is no difference between the two. Thus, dharma cannot be put into words because any spoken words are as good as unspoken, and silence speaks just as loudly. This is the supreme perfect enlightenment that is the perfection of the true reality of all dharmas, and it is also the realized state of Mahamudra.

The *Heart Sutra* speaks of "the greatest mantra," "the brightest mantra," "the highest mantra," and "the mantra that removes all suffering." That mantra points to this level of spirituality.

I met the Eight Youths, and they related the four levels of Mahamudra to me. If you should believe and uphold these words, then you are indeed a practitioner of Buddhism and a true cultivator of Vajrayana.

23. True Significance of the Guru

In this article, the meaning of the word "guru" refers to my own opinion, and is not the general understanding of the public. Basically, it is the personal thought of the Holy Red Crown Vajra Guru.

A true guru should be well versed in doctrines and principles. Not only should he be able to convey his own ideas well, but he should also understand the perspectives of others. Through rational thinking, the guru dwells in the world of rationale. In the rational world, what is right is right, and what is wrong is wrong. The guru upholds complete objectivity.

According to my observations, people view peace and violence as two opposite conditions. Yet, that is a subjective opinion itself. To reach the true state of peace, one must resort to a rational approach. However, human beings are bound by ignorance and respond by impulse. Humans often release their emotions through violence, in which case one loses all rationale.

I always advocate a rational approach employing reason, knowledge, and morality as a means to advance the order of human life. On the personal level, one must build and nurture one's character. When it comes to expounding the truth, it is fruitful if others are convinced through reason. Thus, my judgments about people and matters are based on the foundation of reasoning.

When I teach the Buddha-dharma, it is inevitable to have disagreements with people that have different opinions. When the Buddha was preaching the Buddha-dharma during his time, he had frequent debates with the Brahmin priests and ascetic monks. I think that all arguments arising from reasoning must also be settled in the domain of reason. The approach to resolving problems thus lies with reason.

The guru is the embodiment of non-anger and non-aggression. His qualities of generosity and tolerance are meant to teach human beings how to resolve negativity. In Sakyamuni Buddha's previous lifetimes, there are accounts of how he saved the lives of eagles and tigers by feeding them with his flesh and body, and he showed no resentment towards people who criticized and hurt him.

I strongly feel that the source of all human disputes are the result of "negativity," which then turns into hatred. This is the ignorance of sentient beings, manifesting as a strong attachment to the individual ego. Thus, as the guru teaches the Buddha-dharma, he wants to actualize the path of reason, for any dispute can be resolved through rational exchange, and it is not necessary to resort to violence. Buddha-dharma is about respect for life, offering compassion to all beings, and certainly not killing them!

When the guru is engaged in debate, he reasons with kindness and forbearance. Yet, he is firm with his reasons, expressed in a steadfast and compelling manner. His intentions and reprimand also arise from deep love. Reprimands are given only to illustrate thoughts of peace and to remove all hatred.

Those who listen to me shall be liberated. Those who do not are unfortunate and without affinity. This is the core principle of why the Holy Red Crown Vajra Master writes to help the sentient beings.

Within the teachings of the Highest Yoga Tantra and Mahamudra, the living guru who transmits the Mahamudra is tantamount to being the manifestation of Sakyamuni Buddha himself. When we respect and honor the guru, we are also respecting and honoring Sakyamuni Buddha.

An individual who receives this book should repay the guru's aspiration of transmitting the precious dharma by pursuing the path of nirvana, which leads to perfect enlightenment. He should personally cultivate the practice and set an example for others to follow. The Tantric lineages holders have clearly taught us that the light of one's heart is the manifestation of the guru, when the guru is not physically around. Practitioners should apply Mahamudra in actual practice. By doing so, your heart is your illumination and your refuge. You should treat the brilliance of your heart as your own guru. You must depend on yourself to practice and actualize Mahamudra, for no guru can walk on the path for you; only you can do this for yourself.

The Highest Yoga Tantra and Mahamudra is a supreme dharma that pervades the entire dharma realm. It is one teaching that encompasses many other dharmas. Once the practitioner gains spiritual union with Mahamudra, he will understand the power of it and realize the true significance of the guru. Fundamentally speaking, "mi gnas pa'i," which means non-abiding, points to the fact that there is no end to the practice of cultivation, and that there is no differentiation between the enlightened individual, the state of samsara, and the state of nirvana.

It is crucial that the guru does not enter into parinirvana, and is willing to stay in samsara to benefit all sentient beings. The guru blesses people with his strenuous bodhi effort. He exercises the omnipresent power of great compassion shared by all buddhas and bodhisattvas in his actions, guiding people towards the path of the highest virtues. The guru is the light of realized wisdom, and his nature combines with that of the practitioner to become one. This is where the benefits and bliss of Mahamudra lie, for the light of the guru holds incredible and supreme spiritual power.

In the past, people have asked me, "Why does the guru live in such agony? Isn't it a torment to write books and expound the Dharma?"

I replied, "So long as there are sentient beings remaining to be delivered, then I must continue to write and preach the dharma. It is only when all sentient beings have been succored that I will stop."

"Why is guru here on earth?"

"I came here out of my bodhisattva compassion for sentient beings."

As a guru, my fundamental position is to establish a bodhisattva cultivation ground on earth through the actual practice of Buddhism. By establishing the images of a bodhisattva and a vajra, we are able to carry out these roles through the rational approach. When we exercise compassion, we are exercising reason. We also use reason to subjugate all mara beings.

At present, True Buddha School has forty thousand disciples [this number was based on the total number of disciples as of 1984, when this book was written]. In the future, more will join, indicating the growth of compassion. The school relies on the "True Buddha" as its guiding principle, who advocates the altruistic bodhisattva path and propagates the dharma so that people can benefit from increased wisdom and blessings. This is the true significance of the guru.

The Holy Red Crown Vajra Master is a genuine authentic Vajra Acarya. I once said that a Tantric master should have the following four manifestations:

> Svabhavikakaya, the Essence Body - All prevailing as the universal realm of space, the Mother. May sentient beings invoke the presence of the Svabhavikakaya of the Master.

> Dharmakaya, the Truth Body - All prevailing as the univer-

sal realm of space, the Mother. May sentient beings invoke the presence of the Dharmakaya of the Master.

Sambhogakaya, the Reward Body - All prevailing as the universal realm of space, the Mother. May sentient beings invoke the presence of the Sambhogakaya of the Master.

Nirmanakaya, the Transformation Body - All prevailing as the universal realm of space, the Mother. May sentient beings invoke the presence of the Nirmanakaya of the Master.

Let me say this:

A true authentic guru has cultivated for many lifetimes. His virtues are complete and perfect, and he remains spiritually free. His accomplishments are extraordinary and he has gained great wisdom. He is able to attain all dharma while living on earth and does not have to wait until his death before gaining his attainment. He is endowed with the great power of the Mahamudra of Meditative Absorption. He has also entered into the Ocean of Vairocana and has realized all dharma.

Indeed, the guru has accomplished the highest level of spirituality and according to the Buddha, he will surely attain Buddhahood. With the great spiritual power that he has acquired, he will be able to carry on the buddha's mission. Having mastered all of the teachings, he has the ability to discipline and tame the hearts of all sentient beings. He presents himself in a magnificent form and finds complete freedom in both the mundane and transcendental worlds. He is indeed a supreme sage who is able to manifest himself into countless bodies, which pervade all space. He is the Great Seal, which is the nature of Emptiness itself. His manifested forms are perfect and complete, and since he is in tune with the original body of Buddha-nature, he suitably appears to sentient beings when the need arises. Sentient beings can rely on him, as his compassion is indiscriminate. His diamond nature is indestructible, and his merits are as expansive as the ocean. He expounds the Dharma to deliver sentient beings, and takes in all who are lost, offering them wisdom by revealing the meaning of truth. He speaks the absolute truth and no mara can ever defeat him.

When we want to truly understand the "true significance of the guru," we must begin with these two words: compassion and wisdom. Master Ouyang Chingwu [1871-1943] once said, "It is through compassion that merit becomes significant, and it is through wisdom that merit is accomplished." Everything begins with bodhicitta, as one sets one's mind on the attainment of the supreme perfect enlightenment, so that one may benefit all sentient beings.

To benefit all sentient beings, one must learn to use different forms of wisdom that have different functions. Wisdom derives from the functions of "listening," "thinking," and "cultivating."

When the guru transmits the teachings of Mahamudra, he integrates the Great Mirror Wisdom, the Equanimity Wisdom, Discriminatory Awareness Wisdom, and the All-Accomplishment Wisdom. He combines these forms of wisdom in his transmission. By having great compassion yet lacking great wisdom, there will never be any accomplishment. The same applies for having great wisdom yet lacking great compassion. In that case, nothing is done for the sake of benefitting all sentient beings. Therefore, the broad propagation of Buddha-dharma can only be perfectly accomplished by a guru who is endowed with great compassion and great wisdom.

Hence, herein lies the reason why it is so important for the practitioner to take the Fourfold Refuge, and practice the Guru Yoga. One's gurus include the past lineage holders, the living guru, and one's own heart. These three merge into one and become indivisible.

When one practices the Guru Yoga, the power of the meritorious blessings of the guru dissolves into the individual.

When one practices the Guru Yoga, one recognizes that the guru and one are undivided in essence.

When one practices the Guru Yoga, one cuts through the attachment of self and others. It is of utmost importance.

24. Affection Practice of Ragaraja

When I was touring Japan, I encountered a unique vidyaraja [wisdom king] statue. This statue had two heads, a left
wrathful face and a right benevolent face, and was enthroned on a
red lotus. I asked the temple abbot about the name of this statue and
I was told that it was Ragaraja [Aizen in Japanese], an embodiment of
Acala and Ragaraja. He was well revered for his great vow of bestow-
ing respect and affection.

Later, I learned that Ragaraja also appears in a two-headed or sin-
gle-head form with six arms, each of which carries a ritual imple-
ment. His most significant implements are the bow and arrow. When
he shoots at the hearts of sentient beings, he brings them love and
passion. Also, Ragaraja has three eyes, and sits on a blossoming lotus.

Later on when my master passed the teaching to me, I learned that
although Ragaraja appears wrathful on the outside, he is actually quite
the opposite on the inside. Due to his affectionate and loving nature,
he surpasses all other vidyarajas. If a man yearns for a woman, he
should write the word "female" and place the note in the vidyaraja's
hand. If a woman desires a man, she should write the word "male" and
place it in thr vidyaraja's hand. Their wishes will then be fulfilled. The

amazing effect is due to the original vow that Ragaraja made to bring respect and affection to devotees.

There are couples who are in strained relationships or husbands and wives in shaky marriages. There are also men who seek women, and women who seek men. Therefore, I taught them the affection practice of Ragaraja, and they received swift and wonderful responses as a result! This mystical ritual, together with the original vow of Ragaraja, yields the most supreme dharma power.

For the sake of desperate singles looking for companions or distressed couples needing to patch things up in their relationships, I have decided to disclose the Ragaraja Affection Practice:

The practitioner must first enshrine the image or statue of Ragaraja. The one-headed and six-armed Ragaraja is portrayed as follows: He is red and white in color. He has three fearsome eyes, five-colored hair knots extending to his ears, and a lion's crown adorned on his head. He has six arms. The first of his left arms holds a vajra bell, the second arm holds a bow, and the third and lowest arm holds a lotus flower. The first of his right arms holds a five-pronged vajra, the second arm holds an arrow, and the third arm also holds a lotus flower. He is seated on a red lotus throne. The practitioner may find an artist to paint an image of Ragaraja, or ask a sculptor to carve his statue.

Next, one should collect 108 stamens from red lotus flowers as an offering. In addition, one should offer various delicacies to the deity.

Then perform the Fourfold Refuge, the Great Homage, the Mandala Offering, and the Four Immeasurables.

Form the Root Mudra of Ragaraja: The two hands clasp inwardly like a vajra fist, except for the middle fingers that stand up while crossing each other. Form the mudra first before commencing the visualization.

Visualize flame surrounding the body of Ragaraja while he is descending from the sunlight. Visualize the one you love appearing in the flame. Visualize Ragaraja pulling the arrow, which is aimed at the heart of one's loved one.

Recite the mantra of Ragaraja: "Om mo-he-luo fu-ri-luo se-ni-sha fu-ri-luo sa-dan-fu re-ou-hu." [Sanskrit: OM MAHARAGA VAJROS-NISA VAJRASATTVA JAH HUM BAN HOH.]

Recite this mantra 108 times or 1080 times, counting the recitation with your mala beads.

Meditate and enter into samadhi, wherein the practitioner and the loved one join together with the heart of Ragaraja.

After exiting meditative absorption, the practitioner recites the dedication of merits and beseeches Ragaraja to keep his vows of respect and affection.

After performing the Great Homage, take the 108 strands of red lotus stamen and burn them along with sandalwood incense powder in front of the statue of Ragaraja. Once you begin doing this yoga, even if it is only for one night, you will receive marvelous results.

Some people may want to request a sculptor to carve a small statue of Ragaraja out of white sandalwood, that is about the length of one's finger. After enshrining the statue at their altar, they may carry the statue with them wherever they go. By doing that, their endeavors will be successful, and people will respect and support them.

On my path of practicing Vajrayana, many sentient beings have requested my help. Some people's marriages are broken and they suffer from afflictions in their family relationships. Some people are betrayed by their loved ones and they harbor hatred and anger as a result. Because I empathize with these people, I have decided to publicly reveal this supreme teaching in my book. With this practice, I hope that those who practice according to the method outlined here will benefit from it. However, remember that this practice is meant for those who are sincere and honest. The practice will be ineffective for people with evil motives.

This practice will never work for a flirtatious married woman who desires another man.

It will never work for a married man or a man with a girlfriend who craves another woman.

It will never work for a prostitute that has ill intentions to catch a rich man.

It will never work for a man with a fickle heart and whose actions lack integrity. Although they may speak of love, they actually desire sex.

Here is a verse:

> Supreme Ragaraja!
> His merits and vows are unyielding.
> When the heart is sincere, love will be as strong as golden rock,
> Pray to him and you will be blessed with pure light.
> Your relationship will be bestowed with love and respect.
> As the self-nature dissolves into the realm of affectionate beings,
> All hindrances shall be eliminated.
> The true loved ones will be brought together.

I feel that relationship problems have become increasingly chronic in our times. Many men and women are unfaithful, resulting in a high divorce rate throughout the world. Apart from citing incompatibility, the issue of beauty versus ugliness enters the picture. I once had a friend who was deeply attracted to the beauty of women. After they got married, he met another woman who was even more beautiful. As a result, he fell in love with the second woman because he no longer considered his wife to be attractive, and so he kept his distance from her.

According to the Buddhist teachings, beauty and ugliness are illusory, and one mustn't be attached to either. Most people will be attracted to a pretty woman, and this may bring multiple relationships into her life. On the other hand, many people stay away from an ugly woman and thus, she may never get married. The Buddha-dharma says that though there may be women who are born ugly, they may be kind and talented. These women are gold nuggets among the grains of sand. Like a lotus flower that grows out of the mud, these women are completely uncontaminated and their virtue is unmatched by the most beautiful women.

The true Buddha-dharma is depicted in the statement, "form does not differ from emptiness; emptiness does not differ from form." It can certainly be described as "form itself is emptiness; emptiness itself is form." This means that "when one sees form as emptiness, one attains great wisdom. When one sees emptiness as form, one gains great compassion." Thus, I wrote this article based on the compassion of seeing form.

However, I want to instill wisdom in sentient beings. We must know that all beautiful appearances are inherently empty, and subject to the laws of birth and extinction. No woman can preserve her beauty forever. This is like the trees that shed their leaves, and leave their trunks bare and empty in the winter. When I lived in Taiwan, I often travelled across the country to help people find burial sites that had good feng shui. Having seen and examined many places, I could not help but feel melancholy at what I saw. The beautiful women had become heaps of bones. After the bones were exhumed, they were arranged and stacked in an urn. When you look at a skull that has two hollows for eyes, a nasal cavity, and an opening between the upper and lower jaws, where does the beauty lie?

Hence, what appears as beautiful and hideous is really the same thing, and there is not much of a difference at all.

What is pure and what is impure? In the realm of impermanent phenomena, where the self is non-existent, there is no differentiation between what is impure and pure, for these things are illusory. Those who practice the Highest Yoga Tantra and Mahamudra must understand this principle.

Our bodies will perish one day, and all that is attractive and unattractive boils down to the same thing. The only thing that matters is the mind and spirit. Those who practice Mahamudra shall attain Buddhahood, and those who do not will end up as ashes. Their minds and spirits will be drawn towards reincarnation in the six realms by the pull of their karma.

Such is the reality where all phenomena arise and cease according to their respective causes and conditions. Knowing this truth, we must exercise both compassion and wisdom.

25. Yoga of Great Secret Accomplishment

One time, a Russian fellow asked his friend to write a letter to me on his behalf, expressing his wish to learn the Vajrayana teachings from me. I gave it much thought before deciding to turn him down. The first reason is due to the fact that he lives in the outskirts of Russia, so he would be unable to receive the necessary empowerment in person. Since he only speaks Russian, there would be a communication gap between us and each dharma transmission would have to rely on the help of a translator. Second, none of my disciples live in his vicinity. Thus, no one would be able to transmit the teachings to him on my behalf. Consequently, there was no benefit in accepting a disciple by name only.

In America, I personally teach and demonstrate the Vajrayana rituals to the western students. When it is necessary, disciples of mine with doctorate degrees translate specific Buddhist terms to these students. All of them also receive the empowerments personally from me. Now that my reputation has travelled to Russia, there would be many difficulties regarding the language barrier when a Russian wants to learn the Tantric practices.

Mr. Haruki Kadokawa, a Japanese entrepreneur who owns a large publishing company called Kadokawa Shoten Publishing, read my book *A Modern Chinese Immortal* in Japanese, and has expressed interest in publishing all of my works. He also wishes to study Vajrayana. However, I only know a little Japanese. I would have to rely on my father as a translator, and he would have to fly from Taiwan to Japan. Then I would have to fly from the United States to meet Mr. Kadokawa in Japan before I could properly transmit the secret teachings to him.

Though I did not agree to transmit the teachings to the Russian fellow, he was persistent. He continued to write letters to his friend. Finally, I decided to transmit a mantra and mudra to him so that he could cultivate. The mantra was translated phonetically from Tibetan into Chinese, from Chinese into English, and then finally into Russian. I drew a picture of the mudra and taught him how to use it during his practice.

The method that I taught him was the Yoga of Great Secret Accomplishment, the Yoga of Bodhisattva Vajracakra.

I once said that according to Tantric rules, all official students of Vajrayana are required to take refuge and receive the empowerment. All mudras and mantras must be transmitted from the guru, and they should not be practiced through mere learning from a book. If one has not entered the mandala to receive the appropriate empowerment and one casually forms the mudra or performs the practice, it is tantamount to stealing the dharma and there will be no accomplishments in any practices that one does.

The word secret is associated with the Vajrayana teachings, which is also called the Secret Sect, because a lengthy period of time is required to properly teach and elucidate the recitations and sadhanas in stages. Most people without the capacity for great wisdom are unable to accept and uphold the vastness of these sadhanas. This is why initiates must take refuge first, receive the appropriate empowerment and then receive the proper guidance from the master.

However, there was no vajra master in his area, and he was too far away. In addition, there was a communication barrier. Sakyamuni Buddha had specially transmitted a method for the sake of these sentient beings, known as the Yoga of Cakravajradhara [Mahacakravajra]. This practice is stated as follows:

Enshrine a statue of Sakyamuni Buddha. Prostrate before the Buddha and make precious offerings. Form the Mudra of Cakravajradhara, as follows: The fingers of both hands are crossed and interlocked inwardly, except for the index fingers which stand erect, and the two middle fingers wrap around the top section of the index fingers. The thumbs point straight up and lean on the index fingers.

While forming the mudra, clearly visualize Sakyamuni Buddha approaching you with a vase to give you an empowerment. Recite the Mantra of Cakravajradhara 21 times:

"Namo shi-di-li-ye di-wei-jia-nan sa-fu-da-ta dai-nan-du wei-luo-ni-wei-luo-ni mo-ha-zuo-jie-luo fu-ri-li sa-dai-sa-dai sa-luo-di-sa-luo-di da-luo-yi-da-luo ni-tuo-me-ni san-pan-re-ni da-luo-me-di shi-tuo-ni-li-da-lan soha."

[Sanskrit: NAMAH STRIYA-DHIVIKANAM TATHAGATANAM OM VIRAJI VIRAJI MAHACAKRA-VAJRI SATA SATA SARATE SARATE TRAYI TRAYI VIDHAMANI SAMBHANJANI TRAMATI SIDDHA-GRIYA TRAM SVAHA]

While sitting in meditation, visualize yourself entering into the heart of Sakyamuni Buddha.

Once this practice is applied, one gains accomplishment in one's practice of all Tantric teachings and enters into all mandalas. If one lives in a remote and inconvenient place where no master can be found, where communication is hindered by language barriers, and where empowerment cannot take place, this Yoga of Great Secret Accomplishment is beneficial. This is indeed the most secretly transmitted expedient approach.

However, when a master is available, there is no language barrier, and it is convenient for you to seek an empowerment and the dharma transmission from a master, then there is no justification for you to use this method. If you resort to using this method and refuse to seek the dharma from a master or take refuge in him, then you will not attain union in any of your practices.

Someone said to me, "Master Lu, you have revealed the most secret practice, which is the Five Secret Heart Essence. This is indeed remarkable. Even the unspeakable Cakra-vajradhara Practice has been revealed. Revelation of such Vajrayana practices will certainly cause people to awaken their faith when they learn about them. But, why is it that people still disbelieve you and slander you?"

"Ha! Ha!" I laughed, and said, "There is nothing surprising about people who doubt and slander me. This is like the woodpecker that is only aware of the food in front of it when it pecks the wood, and the maggot that knows no joy except by wriggling in feces. It is like people who crave to be government officials but find no happiness aside from the political life they lead. Thus, the deaf cannot hear the dharma sound, and the blind cannot read the wonderful dharma that I write. Those who doubt and slander me are like this."

While writing this book on Mahamudra, I have literally revealed sixty percent of the realization and experiences attained in my cultivation. Other scriptures rarely go into such detailed elucidation of Mahamudra practices, which makes this book extremely special. As I write this book on the practices of Mahamudra, all of the bodhisattvas extend their respect to me and one buddha commented, "When one accepts and upholds the Mahamudra teachings, it is as good as being close to me and being one with me. This is the purest dharma seal in the universe."

This is the Highest Yoga Tantra, the Formless Gate that has no boundaries. I remember a verse from the Avatamsaka Sutra, that states that the level of great dharma is so high that it is difficult for most people to believe in. Perhaps it is due exactly to its greatness and supremacy that most mundane mortals find the highest dharma difficult to believe in and understand.

The verse goes like this:

> Striving for the Great Vehicle is still easy
> Compared to the greater difficulty of believing in this teaching.
> Even more difficult is it to retain, recite, and explain it to others.
> To practice according to the teaching and truly understand it.
> To hold a galaxy in one's head
> Without moving for an eon,
> Is not considered difficult
> Compared to believing in this teaching.
> To pick up ten buddha-lands in your hand
> And stand in space for an eon
> Is not considered to be hard
> Compared to believing in this teaching.
> If one provides comforts for an eon
> To the homes of beings as numerous as the atoms in ten lands,
> One's merit is not considered as supreme.
> One who believes in this teaching is most excellent.
> Even if one spends an eon serving
> As many buddhas as there are atoms in ten lands,
> The merit of reciting and upholding this book,
> Is far greater and more supreme.

There is another version of the Mantra of Cakravajradhara as follows:

"Namo shi-di- li-ye-di-wei-jia-nan sa-fu-da-ta mu-dai-nan om ri-fu-luo-ni niang-jie-luo-sa-ye soha" [Sansrkit: NAMA STRIYA-DH-VIKANAM SARVA TATHAGATANAM OM VAJRAGNA AKAR-

SAYA SVAHA]

You can choose to recite either of these two mantras.

You may visualize the spot located four finger lengths below the solar plexus chakra, which gives rise to the fire of wisdom, burning away all discursive thoughts. When all impurities are cleansed, the mind is like space, where the purified self merges with the pure dharma realm. By approaching our cultivation in this way, one is able to gain a response in every practice.

Someone asked me, "Lian-sheng, are you really the king of mantras?"

I said, "I do not wish to be addressed by the title 'king,' simply because it is associated with a mundane king. A mundane 'king' is subject to the law of birth and death; a king is restrained by territories; a king has to face hindrances in his path. Though he is dignified with a royal status, he is not exempt from the worries and troubles of life." I continued, "Mahamudra yields spiritual powers from samadhi, where one is able to freely comprehend all religious teachings and dogmas. Such is the state of no obstacles, which separates the true reality from the gross reality. Mahamudra is the ultimate of all dharmas, the king of all kings, but this should not be viewed in the context of a worldly king."

The dharma of all dharmas and the king of all kings, is established within the pure realm of Emptiness.

It is "Truth" itself.

The primordial consciousness of the universe can never be contaminated by the grossness of the five elements.

26. Mantra of Vajrapani Bodhisattva

There is a heavenly secret hidden within this article. Those who are able to perceive it have a spiritual connection, and those who do not perceive it do not.

Hidden within this article is a mystery that holds the secret to all Vajrayana teachings. Thus, anyone who is willing to practice this method is truly blessed.

Someone once asked me, "Who is Vajrapani?"

I replied, "Only I can answer you."

"How pompous of you!"

"I am not being arrogant. I truly know the answer."

"Don't other practitioners know?"

"If they are not enlightened, then they wouldn't really know." I laughed loudly.

Today, if anyone should ask me who Vajrapani really is, I will pose the same question to them and ask, "Who is Vajrapani?"

Someone told me that Vajrapani Bodhisattva is Vajra Heart Bodhisattva (Mahasthamaprapta Bodhisattva).

Someone told me that Vajrapani is Vairocana Buddha.

Someone told me that Vajrapani is Samantabhadra Bodhisattva.

Someone told me that Vajrapani is Trailokyavijaya.

Someone told me that Vajrapani is Vajrasattva.

Today, let me tell you who Vajrapani really is. Vajrapani ranks among the eight major bodhisattvas and he is regarded as the Vajra Holder, who is the Lord of Secrets. As his identity is the Lord of Secrets, few people know who he truly is. Accounts of his identity, as described in the scriptures, are vague. It is stated that while dwelling in the Diamond Mandala, Vairocana manifested and merged into the Samadhi Absorption of Samantabhadra. Then he manifested a great and round moon-like light, which became the body of Vajrapani. This light is the perfect bodhi heart seal.

Amidst the moonlight there is a glowing vajra. Vajrapani is the combined entity of Samantabhadra Bodhisattva and Vajrasattva.

Vajrapani is the supreme dharma prince of all Tathagatas, the very bodhicitta of all Tathagatas. He is thus the very supreme master of secrecy of all Tathagatas. Hence he is given the title, the Vajra Holder, Lord of Secrets. He is depicted with his right hand brandishing a vajra sceptre. His left hand, which extends to his hip, displays a fist or holds a bell. His right hand, which brandishes a vajra, is held close to his heart.

Okay. So who then is Vajrapani Bodhisattva? Is he Vairocana Buddha? Samantabhadra Bodhisattva? Vajrasattva? Vajra Heart Bodhisattva? Trailokyavijaya? Well, he is all of them and yet he is not all of them. Let me keep the suspense up for another minute.

Just look at my dharma form. I wear a five-buddha crown, which represents the five buddhas. My left hand holds a vajra bell and my right hand holds a vajra scepter. I wear a dharma robe and sit on a lotus throne. Now consider the dharma form of the Vajra Holder, Lord of Secrets. His right hand holds a vajra and his left hand holds a bell. His head is adorned with a vajra crown wherein Vairocana Buddha is in the center and he is flanked by the respective buddhas of the north, east, south and west.

So who is this Vajrapani? Let me say this: All enlightened vajra

masters are Vajrapani himself. Vajrapani Bodhisattva is the bodhicitta of all buddhas. Mahasthamaprapta Bodhisattva is the heart of
wisdom. Vajrapani Bodhisattva is the heart secret of all practitioners.
Thus, Vajrapani Bodhisattva is the Vajra Heart Bodhisattva, whose
heart links sentient beings with all buddhas and bodhisattvas.

I would boldly proclaim, "I am Vajrapani," and then point my finger at you and say, "If you attain realization, then you too shall be
Vajrapani."

Thus, a master sees his heart as the heart of Vajrapani Bodhisattva,
and sees his form as the form of Vajrapani Bodhisattva. With that
in mind, he propagates the teachings of Vajrayana. This is the true
meaning of Vajrayana. This is the true meaning of the Vajra Holder,
Lord of Secrets, as seen through the dharma form of the Holy Red
Crown Vajra Guru, the Venerable Tantric Master Lian-sheng.

Here is a transmission of the Mantra Recitation of Vajrapani Bodhisattva.

1. Form the Mudra of Vajrapani.
2. Visualize that Vajrapani is surrounded by a halo of white
   light.
3. Visualize a beam of white light radiating from the third
   eye of Vajrapani towards the practitioner's third eye.
4. Recite the mantra, "Om po-ri-luo sa-da-po er [Sanskrit:
   OM VAJRASATTVA AH]" 108 times or 1080 times.

One performs the practice by following the standard procedures
outlined in the sadhana practice book. With the mantra, mudra and
visualization, along with a great mandala, one can proceed to enter
into the samadhi of Samantabhadra and ultimately, attain the samadhi of Vajrasattva. At that time, one receives the buddhas' blessing
and attains the Infinite Dharani Gate of the Infinite States of Samadhi.
When one identifies with the incomprehensible dharma power, one is
transformed into Vajrapani.

This practice also involves the manifestation of the vajra seed within the Alaya consciousness. Once the practitioner receives the dharma transmission of the Five Wisdoms, he becomes Vajrapani himself.

Vajrapani uses the moon disc of the heart to lovingly bestow blessings upon sentient beings by reciting the following mantra: Om mo-he-mei-di-li soha [Sanskrit: OM MAHA MAITRYI SPHARA].

Vajrapani uses the moon disc of the heart to compassionately liberate sentient beings from suffering, by reciting the following mantra: Om mo-he-jia-lu-na-ye soha [Sanskrit: OM MAHA KARUNAYA SPHARA].

Vajrapani uses the moon disc of the heart to joyously transmit the dharma to sentient beings, by reciting the following mantra: Om sa-po-shi tuo-ben-luo-mo na-sa-po-luo [Sanskrit: OM SARVA SUDDHA PRAMODA SPHARA].

Vajrapani uses the moon disc of the heart to equanimously bestow bodhicitta upon sentient beings, by reciting the following mantra: Om mo-hu bi-qi-sa soha [Sanskrit: OM MAHOPEKSA SPHARA].

During the practice, the master recites each of the four mantras above 108 times, as outlined in the dharma instructions. Whatever the sentient beings wish for, the vajra master bestows their requests. Since a genuine vajra master dwells in samadhi and practices the Vajrapani sadhana, he is able to grant the wishes of sentient beings.

By engaging in the Vajrapani practice, one will be able to see Vajrapani whose light is brilliant. By forming the mudra, the practitioner can hide in the light and gain complete freedom. Such an accomplishment is certainly extraordinary.

Additionally, when one immerses into samadhi, the mantras can treat every affliction and one can gain accomplishment in all Karma [action] Practices. Thus,when one attains accomplishment in the samadhi, all prayers and requests will naturally be answered.

Today, my elucidation of the great teaching of the Vajra Holder, Lord of Secrets, manifested from the Tathagata. These mantras are spoken by the throne holder and they are precious words. When sentient beings are faced with calamities, Vajrapani arrives to succour them. When one practices this teaching, all situations involving possession by spirits, illness, disharmony in the family, or major calamities, will improve due to the merits of recitation. [If one does not practice this teaching], then the individual should quickly seek the help from an authentic vajra master to help him out of his predicament.

Here is a verse in praise of Vajrapani:

> From the buddha heart comes the dharma rain.
> From the wisdom moon, the rays of compassion shine.
> Vajrapani with his vajra scepter
> Is indeed the Lord of Secrets.

Who is Vajrapani? He is the bodhicitta of all Tathagatas. When sentient beings put this into practice, they shall gain response with Vajrapani.

Without temperance through hardships, how can one attain true accomplishment?

Sheng-yen Lu

27. A Brief Introduction to the Vajrayana Sadhanas

How many sadhanas are there in Vajrayana Buddhism? I would say the number is infinite. The Buddha traditionally categorized myriads of sadhanas into 84,000 dharma methods, which in reality are as numerous as the sands of the Ganges River.

Many people have asked me how they should begin their cultivation in this ocean of Tantric teachings. My answer is that it would be best to focus on one sadhana and advance in sequence, from the lowest level to the highest one. One should focus on the depth of one's concentration during each session. When you concentrate, you will surely feel spiritual responses.

Someone once asked me, "Master Lu, do you understand all of the 84,000 dharma methods?"

I replied that the Holy Red Crown Vajra Guru has been cultivating for many lifetimes and has attained realization. Thus I know all teachings and there is no Tantric teaching that is beyond my understanding. This is especially true when I perform a ritual. I am able to ascertain its truth and gain attainment. The supreme cosmic consciousness becomes one with me and I become one with the supreme cosmic consciousness, for there is no difference between both. Therefore, I can say that all teachings have flowed from my heart into the world, and all teachings trace their origins back to me. So, how can I not understand them?

The Vajrayana teachings are wide-ranging. In Tibet, there are the Four Tibetan Schools, namely the Nyingmapa, Gelugpa, Kagyupa, and Sakyapa. The Tantric Buddhism that was propagated from Mount Tiantai during the Tang Dynasty of China is known as Chinese Vajrayana. The Tantric Buddhism propagated by Kukai of Japan is known as Japanese Vajrayana [Shingon Buddhism].

Anyone who wishes to practice Vajrayana Buddhism must first take refuge and receive empowerment from a guru. It is only with the guru's reliance that one can begin to cultivate the Vajrayana practices.

The master who transmits the teachings of True Buddha School is the Holy Red Crown Enlightened Vajra Acharya. His system of practice is briefly stated as follows:

1. The Four Preliminaries
2. The Padmakumara Yoga (Guru Yoga)
3. Personal Deity Yoga. The personal deity is the deity that an individual has the greatest affinity with in his cultivation.
4. The Five Vajra Practices or the Practices of the Eight Vidyarajas.
5. Highest Yoga Tantra and Meditative Absorption Practice of Mahamudra

Among the Tantric dharma methods, the Nyingma School has the greatest collection of practices. The Holy Red Crown Vajra Guru has integrated the various teachings of Nyingmapa, Gelugpa, Kagyupa, Sakyapa, Chinese Vajrayana, and Japanese Vajrayana. I shall briefly introduce the sadhana that I have been cultivating:

The Four Preliminaries, which include the Fourfold Refuge, the Great Mandala Offering, the Great Homage, and the Vajrasattva Practice.

The Yoga of Padmakumara (this True Buddha School practice must be cultivated by every True Buddha disciple).

I have practiced many personal deity yogas, which include the following: the Yogas of Sakyamuni, Sitatapatra, Vipulagrabhe Maniprabhe Tathagata, Padmasambhava, Medicine Buddha, Manjushri Bodhisattva, Avalokitesvara Bodhisattva, White Tara, Green Tara, Twenty-one Taras, Amitabha Buddha, Arhat, Maitreya Bodhisattva, Vairocana Tathagata, Aksobhya Buddha, Ratnasambhava, Amoghasiddhi, Buddha Locana, Cundi Bodhisattva, Mahamayuri Vidyarajni, Akasagarbha, Mahamati, Dipamkara, Prabhutaratna, Mahasthamaprapta, Samantabhadra, Ksitigarbha, Suryaprabha, Candraprabha, Mahapratisara, Bhaisajyaraja, and so forth.

The Five Heruka Yogas and the Eight Vidyaraja Yogas [of the Nyingmapa Mahayoga] include the following: the Yogas of Yamantaka, Hevajra, Cakrasamvara, Ucchusma, Kalachakra, Acala, Vajrahumkara, Kundah, Vidyottama, Ragaraja, Mahamayuri Vidyarajni, Hayagriva, Aparajitah, the Five Vidyarajas of Great Power, Atavaka, Trailokyavijaya, Padanaksipa, Vajrahasa, Mahachakra, and so forth.

The Yogas of the Highest Yoga Tantra and Mahamudra include the following: the Yogas of Phowa, Inner Fire[Tummo], Light Drops, Ekagrata, Tranquility and Contemplation, Supreme Bliss, Immovability, Clear Light, Consciousness Transference, Forceful Projection [drongjug], Eternal Rainbow Light, the Yoga of Permanence, Bliss, Self, and Purity, and so forth.

Among these dharma methods there are also many other special yogas, which include the following: the Yogas of Bardo Deliverance, Food Offering, External Yogas, Five Maitreya Tantras, Great Perfection, Lamdre, Vajrakilaya, Seven Treasures of Longchenpa, Essence of Mother and Son Lights, Harmonious Combination and Turning,

Nine Vehicles of Great Round Light, Black Robe Vajra, Great Homa Puja, Internal Yogas, Great Compassionate Mother Tara, Gathering the Light at the Crown, Wish-Fulfilling Lotus and Turning of the Mani Pearl, Great Compassion and Wisdom of Emptiness, Salendraraja, and so forth.

As for the Yogas of the heavenly deities and their retinues, they are listed as follows: The Four Heavenly Kings, Devanam Indra, Brahma, Sri Mahadeva, Marici, Sarasvati, Paranirmitavasavartins, Yamadevas, Aditya, Candra, Prihivi, Varuna, Agni, Vaju, Mahakala, Dharmapala, Mahesvara, Nandikesvara and so forth. The Yogas of these deities are simply countless. Other Yogas belonging to the retinues of the buddhas, the bodhisattvas, the arhats, the devas and the dharma protectors are unique in their own categories.

The Vajrayana yogas that I have mentioned here are the more common ones, and do not constitute all of the yogas I know. However, they constitute the yogas that a master should know. There are still many other secret heart teachings, which I have practiced but have not completely disclosed in writing. You must be wondering how a forty-year old person like me could have possibly studied so many sadhanas. Could it be possible at all? Do not be surprised! I have been practicing the Tantric teachings for many, many lifetimes. Without such a foundation, how would I dare profess that I am the Holy Red Crown Vajra Guru, the Venerable Tantric Master?

Besides knowing the proper yogas, I also know how to defend the evil yogas of the Black Sect, which include the following: the Arts of Moon in Water, Killing by Thoughts, Destroying Boundary Protection, Darkness, Erotic Seduction, Black Water, Spreading Malaria Overnight, Devious Wisdom, Five Poisons, Sexual Union, Lustful Bliss, Flooding, Hailstorm, Solar Eclipse, Lunar Eclipse, Flying through Space, Evil Transformation, Substitution, Love Spells, and so forth.

I feel that if an adept wants to become a master and transmit the dharma, he should shoulder demanding responsibilities, excel through hardships in cultivation, and pass the great mara tests. Without temperance through hardships, how can one attain true accomplishment?

Thus, once the disciples of True Buddha School have clearly set their goals, they should commit themselves to practice and gradually, perfect realization will radiate from within.

Sheng-yen Lu

28. Conclusion to the *Highest Yoga Tantra and Mahamudra*

What really is the Highest Yoga Tantra? Since there is no secret greater than the secret of this tantra, that makes it the Highest Yoga Tantra. Therefore, it is truth itself.

What then is Mahamudra? It is the true reality itself. It is an approach that explains the truth of reality in all completeness.

As a vajra master, I have practiced the Meditative Absorption of Mahamudra diligently. I regard cultivation with a serious attitude and have built up a solid foundation. The Highest Yoga Tantra and Mahamudra book summarizes the essence of my realization.

I feel that I have elaborated the teachings in this book in great detail. However, I know that there will be some people who will find this book incomprehensible. In that case, it is not surprising that they do not understand this work since this is, after all, the Highest Yoga Tantra. Those who do not understand this book should seek guidance from a vajra master to clarify the text. Those who wish to practice it should request the appropriate empowerment from a master, and practice accordingly. If there is any unclear area or step, the practitioner should seek clarification from a master. Anyone who gains accomplishment with the Highest Yoga Tantra and Mahamudra will certainly attain Buddhahood. Hence, within the pages of this book lies the great secret of attaining Buddhahood. One who receives this book is truly blessed and has a great affinity.

More and more people in this world are taking interest in Vajrayana teachings. This interest stems from our subconscious, which is naturally attracted to the joy of brilliance. However, this supreme teaching of the Highest Yoga Tantra and Mahamudra is usually hidden in secrecy. Some masters would never disclose their heart essence of realization because they regard their realization as a heavenly secret. They guard this secret as their own private treasure. Today, I have revealed my heart essence to the world out of compassion and I risk revealing the celestial secrets. I am the kind of person that is willing to sacrifice my life for the truth.

I want to share with you the true meaning of life. A person must cultivate with the intention to leave material desires behind, thus achieving purification of the self. Otherwise, he will never be able to perceive the true face of truth, no matter how hard he practices and how much he learns.

I also know very well that human beings are the most fortunate of all living things, for they are governed by the mind and spirit. Only human beings are endowed with the blessings of the supreme consciousness; only humans can receive the most precious blessings above all other beings, for humans are given the ability and authority to cultivate. It is only through cultivation that humans can hope to experience the dharma nature of truth itself.

These relationships are explained here:

Human beings - They possess the special gift to return to earth to cultivate (the true meaning of life).

Earth - It is the training ground where human beings cultivate to return to the truth.

Truth - It is another name for the supreme cosmic consciousness, which can be called "buddha."

The nature of joy - It is the quality which moves one towards the light.

The nature of laziness - It is the condition which drags one towards darkness.

Cultivation - One should get rid of laziness and work towards joy. Mitigate the dark deluded thoughts, and move close to the light itself.

The teachings of Mahamudra - They comprise the highest cultivation practices, which help one to realize and attain Buddhahood.

Now that I have clarified these relationships, those who are still trapped by desire should wake up quickly! Why would one waste time indulging in gambling, sex, money, fame, alcohol, or status? Do not become idle and disregard practice. Besides going about your daily routine, you must find some time for cultivation. Do not despair and do not mull over the past. We must strive to enrich ourselves every day. Time flies, like the blink of lightning and sparks. In no time we will become old. Just like lightning and thunder or a burning flame, all phenomena are extinguished as soon as they are created. Once they cease, the phenomena are created again.

There are many detours along the path to seeking truth. We must take the refined spiritual path, and avoid the unpaved road. Temples, spiritual mediums, superficial prostrations, distorted religious teachings, and worldly pleasures are all the products of "mirages." Thus, it is vital to truly nourish one's inner strength and inner light. We should turn towards cultivation as a means to reach the truth. However, along the way we need to differentiate between what is good and what is evil. We may have to experience countless setbacks and disappointments along the way, before we finally arrive at the realm of truth where Buddhahood lies.

Why did I name my school True Buddha School? It is because I have seen too many religious sects promote principles with unrealistic expectations. Some sects speak only about faith, while others only perform rituals. On the one hand, there are teachings that emphasize kindness, reciting the buddha's name, performing prostrations, resolving calamities, and bardo deliverance. However, there are also some religious sects which offer nothing except deception. They cheat people out of their wealth and chastity.

It is for this reason that I decided to combine the strengths of various religious schools into one school and perfect these strengths. Since I combined the best practices of other religious schools into one, and also added the cultivation of the Meditative Absorption of Mahamudra, cultivators will be able to become one with the supreme cosmic consciousness. When one is absorbed in this perfect meditative state, one reaches truth.

Ling - spiritual cultivation. [It refers to the] devotion found in Christianity. [True Buddha School used to be called Ling Xing True Buddha School]

Xian - supreme path of Taoism, including its rituals and teachings.

True - It is the most supreme, and represents the combination of all religious sects. It is the revelation of the self nature, and the union of the self nature with the supreme.

Buddha - It refers to perfect enlightenment, the highest samadhi state of realization and liberation, which constitutes the heart of heart essence of Tantric Buddhism.

Thus, once the disciples of True Buddha School have clearly set their goals, they should commit themselves to practice and gradually, perfect realization will radiate from within. True Buddha School begins with faith, and reaches towards the highest, unexcelled level of accomplishment.

Frankly speaking, the Holy Red Crown Vajra Guru is eternal. He is a master who exists without beginning and without end. This is because he has merged with the supreme truth itself, and has truly attained enlightenment. Truth is infinite, and so is the Holy Red Crown Vajra Guru, who is the perfect master.

I am beyond the confinement of men, gods, and time and space. These three confinements are unable to control me, for my spirit has attained spiritual freedom. Thus I am boundless and infinite. The heart essence that I have realized is the Highest Yoga Tantra and Mahamudra. All the laziness of the past cannot bind me and neither can my past desires tie me down as well. My spirit has attained boundlessness through spiritual liberation, and I have become one with truth itself.

The Holy Red Crown Vajra Guru, Tantric Master Sheng-yen Lu has finally completed the writing of The Highest Yoga Tantra and Mahamudra. Master Sheng-yen Lu is filled with the vibrancy of love, and the fearlessness of the vajra heart. His great compassion in delivering sentient beings and his diligence in practice have made the road ahead of him shine ever brighter. His mind and spirit have entered into the supreme state of joy and bliss.Charged with such great mental power, he shall continue to pave the way, turning himself into the victorious lion king. All disciples of True Buddha School must maintain a state of mental stability and take note of the dharma taste being transmitted. Continue the routine of daily practice, and be grateful to the universal light radiating from the supreme spirits. It is this supreme light, which continuously bestows its great compassion upon humankind.

I am most grateful to Vajradhara (the main name of the Supreme Being).

I am most grateful to Noble Tilopa (the first lineage guru of Kagyupa).

I am most grateful to Noble Naropa (the second lineage guru of Kagyupa).

I am most grateful to Noble Marpa (the third lineage guru of Kagyupa).

I am most grateful to Noble Milarepa (the fourth lineage guru of

Kagyupa).

...... (and to the other lineage holders of Kagyupa).

I thank the Sixteenth Gyalwa Karmapa, Rangjung Rigpe Dorje. He is the spontaneously-manifested and omniscient vajra, who is the guru of Holy Red Crown Vajra Guru. I would also like to thank the many other masters who have taught me.

The lineage of the Meditative Absorption of Mahamudra Practice is supreme. In our daily life, cultivation helps to remove our crude attachment to materialism and refines the self-nature, so that we can radiate light and draw the lineage holders to us through our crown. Through this approach, the individual self is transformed into the universal self and completely merges with the universe.

In this historical moment, the Holy Red Crown Vajra Guru has enabled the Meditative Absorption of Mahamudra to shine in all of its brilliance. This light radiates infinitely throughout eternity. And now the Tantric teachings are destined to be transmitted in the west. In the future, the teaching of Mahamudra shall help the Tantric teachings to flourish, allowing every sentient being the opportunity to be delivered and attain Buddhahood.

May all endeavors be auspicious.

Glossary

-A-

Amitabha Buddha (Sanskrit, literally "Boundless light")
The Buddha of Boundless Light and Longevity, he is one of the Five
Wisdom Buddhas and the Lord of the Lotus Family. He embodies
the Wisdom of Discerning Awareness which is the antidote to desire
and lust. His color is red, element is fire, and direction is west. He is
depicted with his hands forming the meditation mudra. Amitabha
Buddha's pure land (paradise) is called Sukhavati and is located in
the western direction. He is the Primary Buddha of the Pure Land
Sect and often depicted to be accompanied by his two attendants,
Avalokitesvara Bodhisattva and Mahasthamaprapta Bodhisattva.

Amoghavajra (705-774 AD)
A prolific translator who became a politically powerful Buddhist
monk in China, Amoghavajra was born in India and immigrated
to China when he was ten. At fourteen years of age, he became
ordained and studied with Vajrabodhi. After foreign monks were
expelled from China, he traveled to Sri Lanka, India and Southeast
Asia on pilgrimage and met Nagabodhi, the teacher of Vajrabodhi.
He later returned to China with over five hundred volumes of teachings based on the *Tattvasamgraha Tantra* (a central text of Yoga Tantra) of which he translated the first portion. Amoghavajra claimed
to have only translated seventy-seven texts, but many other Chinese
translations are attributed to him. He is acknowledged as one of the
Eight Shingon Patriarchs.

Avalokitesvara (Sanskrit, literally "Lord Who Observes Sounds of the World")
The embodiment of compassion, Avalokitesvara Bodhisattva compassionately observes the sounds of the world and renders assistance to any devotee who calls out his name. The stories of prayers answered and the myriad miracles performed by Avalokitesvara made him the most widely worshipped bodhisattva. Known as Chenrezig in Tibet, the Tibetan people claim to be his descendents and consider him as their patron bodhisattva. They believe that Chenrezig has appeared many times in Tibet to protect the Buddhist faith. King Songtsan Gampo (the Tibetan king who introduced Buddhism into Tibet) and Dalai Lama are believed by Tibetans to be incarnations of Chenrezig. As result of this special relationship, Avalokitesvara's mantra, "Om Mani Padme Hum," is the most widely chanted mantra by the Tibetan people.

Avalokitesvara Bodhisattva is worshipped in China as the female bodhisattva, Guanyin. This change of Avalokitesvara from a male bodhisattva to being depicted as a female one apparently occurred gradually during the Song Dynasty. Some have postulated that Chinese worship Avalokitesvara as a female deity because Chinese culture views compassion as a feminine quality. Guanyin's popularity in China is summed up by the Chinese saying that "The Amitabha Buddha's name is chanted in every house. Guanyin Bodhisattva is worshipped in every home." As Buddhism spread from China into the neighboring Asian countries such as Korea and Japan, Avalokitesvara was introduced to them as Guanyin, a female bodhisattva.

The Buddhist scriptures speak of Avalokitesvara appearing in many forms including the two armed, four armed, or the thousand armed and thousand eyed Avalokitesvara. The scriptures also state that Avalokitesvara will appear in the most suitable form for the circumstances when rendering assistance.

Avatamsaka School (Huayan School)
Unlike most Buddhist schools, this Chinese Buddhist school focuses on the *Avatamsaka Sutra*, also known as the *Flower Adornment Sutra*. The *Avatamsaka Sutra* is one of longest and the most comprehensive compendiums of the Buddhist teachings. It primarily centers on the Buddha's enlightenment and provides a detailed guide for practitioners on the Bodhisattva's Path. The Bodhisattva's Path is presented in four sets of ten stages, culminating with the two levels of enlightenment, the final goal of Mahayana Buddhism.

-B-

Black Sect (Bon)
Considered to be rooted in the indigenous religious tradition of Tibet, it is a system of shamanistic and animistic practices performed by priests called "bonpo." Bon is generally considered to be heretical, and used to perform rituals intended to harm. For this reason, it is generally know as the "Black Sect."

Bodhicitta (Sanskrit, literally "Awakened Mind")
The key to Mahayana Buddhism, it refers both to an enlightened mind and to the resolution arising from the profound compassion to attain an enlightened mind for the purpose of assisting all beings.

Bodhisattva (Sanskrit, literally "Awakened Being")
An enlightened being (or one who has not achieved full enlightenment) who chooses to remain in cyclic existence to assist others to achieve enlightenment.

Bodhisattva Maitreya
He presently resides in the Tushita heaven. He will be the future
buddha of this eon.

Brahma (The Creator)
One of the three primary deities of Hinduism. The other two deities
are Vishnu (the preserver) and Shiva (the destroyer). He is usually
depicted with four heads, four faces, and four arms. Buddhist scriptures recorded that Brahma (called "Indra" in the sutras) appeared
to Shakyamuni Buddha after the Buddha's enlightenment. Brahma
asked the Buddha not to enter nirvana immediately and stay in the
human world to spread Buddha-dharma. Hence, Brahma was the
first who requested the Buddha to "turn the dharma wheel."

Brahmin
A priest of the most privileged caste of the four castes in traditional
Hindu society in India. Originally, this title was given to those who
attained spiritual accomplishment through rigorous practice and
those who adhered to the Vedas. Later on in ancient India, one had
to be born into the Brahmin caste to become a Brahmin priest.

Buddha (Sanskrit, literally "Awakened One")
The term is typically used to refer to the historical Buddha, Shakyamuni Buddha. In Mahayana Buddhism, the term is not restricted to
just Shakyamuni Buddha, but may refers to anyone who is enlightened.

Buddha-dharma
Buddha doctrine or the teachings of the Buddha.

Buddhahood
The stage of enlightenment.

-C-

Chakra (Sanskrit, literally "Wheel")
Seven subtle energy centers in the human body. The root chakra lies
in the area of the sacrum and is said to hold one's dormant energy.
Once awakened, this spiritual energy travels up through the other
five chakras until it reaches the crown chakra at the top of the head.

Channel
In energy physiology of Vajrayana, channels are the energy pathways
which qi and drops travel in the body. There are three main pathways with central channel being the focus of cultivation. The central
channel runs parallel and in front of the spinal cord.

Confucianism
Developed by the Chinese philosopher Confucius (551-478 BC),
this ideology focuses on the cultivation of virtue and maintenance of
ethics and does not involve a belief in the supernatural or a personal
god.

Cultivation
The practices one does in order to purify karma, to purify oneself of
greed, anger, and ignorance, to create merit, to generate bodhicitta
and, ultimately, to achieve enlightenment.

Cundi Bodhisattva
Sometimes referred to as the "Mother of All Buddhas," she is one of
the principal deities of True Buddha School. She is depicted as being
light yellow in color, has eighteen arms and a third eye on her forehead. She is an emanation of Avalokitesvara.

-D-

Deva (Sanskrit, literally "Shining One")
Gods or heavenly beings which, due to their good merit, are able to enjoy the pleasures of heaven. However, they are still trapped in the samsaric cycle and will eventually be reborn in another realm.

Dharani
Originally, it could be a seed syllable, a mantra, a sutra, or a sastra. A practitioner would recite it to help increase memory, increase wisdom, decipher right from wrong, allow one to not be angered, and would teach one the forty-two root seed syllable sounds. In modern times, it is generally referring to a long mantra.

Dharma
Typically, "dharma" is used to describe the body of teachings expounded by the Buddha. However, the word is also used in Buddhist phenomenology as the term for phenomenon, a basic unit of existence and/or experience.

Dharma Protector (Vajra Protector; Wrathful Protector)
An enlightened being that takes on a wrathful form and whose function is to protect Buddhist practitioners.

Dharma Realm
A state of existence, there are ten states of existence: hell denizens, hungry ghosts, animals, asuras, humans, devas, śrāvakas, pratyeka-buddhas, bodhisattvas, and buddhas.

Dharma Wheel
An eight spoke wheel used as a symbol to represent the teachings of Buddhism. "Turning the dharma wheel" means to teach and spread Buddhist teachings.

Dharmakaya (Dharma Body; Truth Body)
One of the three dharma bodies, the dharmakaya body is a manifestation of a buddha that is timeless, formless and is one with the universe. For example, the dharmakaya body of Living Buddha Liansheng is Vairocana Buddha.

Diamond Sutra
An important teaching of Shakyamuni Buddha which shows that all things are ultimately empty and devoid of any inherent reality, including the idea of oneself, other sentient beings, and dharma.

-E-

Eight Shingon Patriarchs
These are: Mahavairocana Buddha, Vajrasattva Bodhisattva, Nagarjuna, Nagabodhi, Vajrabodhi, Amoghavajra, Huiguo, and Kobo Daishi.

Empowerment
A ritual wherein the guru transmits to a student the energy of a particular deity or practice so that the student's practice may quickly bear fruit.

Expedient Means
Methods and teachings to help people understand and bring them closer to authentic dharma, and ultimately bring them to enlightenment. For example, the Jambhala practices entice one to practice to increase their wealth and the result is that one learns Buddhism, the dharma, one's wisdom increases, and, eventually, this individual is brought closer to enlightenment through this expedient practice.

-F-

Five Aggregates (Five Skandhas)
"Skandha" is Sanskrit for "aggregates." The five skandhas are: form, feeling, perception, mental formation, and consciousness. These are psychophysical components of a human being which, when interacting together, create the illusion of self and inherent existence of self.

Five Buddhas
Also known as Five Dhyani Buddhas, the Five Buddhas are celestial buddhas visualized in Vajrayana meditations. The five Buddhas are Aksobhya, Amitabha, Amoghasiddhi, Ratnasambhava and Vairocana. Each embodies a different aspect of enlightened consciousness to aid in spiritual transformation: (1) Vairocana Buddha - Wisdom of Ultimate Reality; (2) Akshobhya Buddha - Wisdom of Great Mirror-like; (3) Ratnasambhava Buddha - Wisdom of Equality in Nature; (4) Amitabha Buddha - Wisdom of Discerning Awareness; (5) Amoghasiddhi Buddha - Wisdom of All-accomplishing.

Five-buddha Crown
Worn by the vajra acharyas of True Buddha School, the crown displays Buddha Vairocana in the center, Buddha Akshobhya in the East, Buddha Ratnasambhava in the South, Buddha Amitabha in the West, Buddha Amogasidhi in the North. Wearing the crown indicates that the vajra acharya is the dharma prince of the Five Direction Buddhas.

Four Preliminaries
These practices remove hindrances and build merit so that one may have greater success in cultivation. They consist of the: (1) the Great Homage; (2) the Mandala Offering; (3) Fourfold Refuge Mantra; (4) Vajrasattva Yoga.

-G-

Gampopa (1079–1153 AD)

Originally a doctor and layman, Gampopa took renunciation in order to calm the mind of his dying wife so that she would not hold onto her life for fear of losing him to another woman. After this, he entered deeply into practice and later found his guru, Milarepa. The teachings of the Kagyu Sect spread widely during the time of Gampopa.

Ganges

A famous river in India which is a pilgrimage site for Hindus because it is believed that bathing in it washes away one's sins, cleanses you of all evil and, if one's ashes are placed in it upon cremation, the river will take you to heaven. It is frequently mentioned in Buddhist sutras since the Buddha spent a lot of time near the Ganges and many Indian people at that time could relate to the metaphors in which he used the Ganges, i.e., "the number sentient beings that would be liberated by the Buddha would be as numerous as the stars that fill the sky, like the sands of the Ganges."

Gelug/Gelugpa/Yellow Sect

Known as the Yellow Sect because of the large yellow hats worn by the reverends during ceremonies, this is the most popular school currently in Tibet and surrounding regions. The founder of Gelug, Tsongkhapa (1367-1419 AD) received teachings from Nyingma, Kaygu, Sakya and other schools. Tsongkhapa was well known for his strict observance of the monastic disciplines as set forth in the Vinaya. In the mid sixteenth century, Sonam Gyatso, the second reincarnation of Tsongkhapa's main disciple was later bestowed the title "Dalai" (Mongolian for "ocean") and the institution of Dalai Lama was created.

Geshe (Tibetan, literally "Virtuous Friend")
Developed in the Sakya Sect, this system is more widely used in the
Gelug Sect, although the Kagyu and Nyingma Sect also have their
own Geshe Curriculum. The title of geshe is given to monks who
have successfully studied the Geshe Curriculum, usually taking
between nine to twenty years. The core of the curriculum consists of
intense study of subjects such as Abhidharma, Prajnaparamita, Mad-
hyamaka (the Middle Way), Pramana (logic), and Vinaya.

Golden Mother of Jade Pond
Ruler of all female immortals, she is the most important female deity of the Taoist Pantheon. Known by many names, such as Queen
Mother of the West, she came into being from the gathering of primordial yin (feminine) energy. Her palace is located on top a peak
in the Kunlun Mountain Range. She represents the metal element in
the Taoist's Five Elements (metal, wood, water, fire, and earth) and
there is a Jade Pond near her palace, hence she is also known as the
Golden Mother of Jade Pond.

Great Perfection
The supreme tantra of the Nyingma School. Cutting Through Resis-
tance (khregs-chod) and All-Surpassing Wisdom (thodgal) are two
of principal practices of Great Perfection. Adepts of Great Perfection
have been known for demonstrating rainbow body accomplishment
upon their passing, in which their flesh bodies gradually dissolves
into five-colored rainbow light leaving hair and nails as the only
physical remains.

Guru
Two Sanskrit words - "gu" means darkness and "ru" means light.
Therefore, a guru is one who can lead the student from darkness to
light - from ignorance to wisdom. In Vajrayana Buddhism, the guru

(teacher) is the first and foremost element of one's level of accomplishment. This teacher gives the practitioner the lineage blessing of all past lineage gurus. The guru has also learned, practiced and attained accomplishments in his or her teachings. With the guidance of an authentic guru, one may more quickly reach enlightenment.

Guru Padmasambhava (Sanskrit, literally "Lotus Born")
Commonly known as the "Second Buddha," after Shakyamuni Buddha. Padmasambhava was supremely accomplished in the esoteric arts and used his powers to defeat many demons and black magic practitioners in Tibet in the eighth century. He is the founder of the Nyingma tradition of Tibetan Buddhism. Padmasambhava is one of the principal deities of True Buddha School.

Guru Pufang
Guru Pufang lived on an island off the coast of Taiwan where he built a temple to honor Mahacundi Buddha Mother, his personal deity.

Guru Thubten Dargye
Vajra Acharya Thubten Dargye of the Gelug School gave the Highest Yoga Tantra empowerment to Living Buddha Lian-sheng, among many other empowerments.

Guru Yoga
In Vajrayana Buddhism, the guru is the embodiment of the Triple Jewels - the Buddha, Dharma and Sangha. To practice the Guru Yoga is to merge with the mind-stream of one's guru, thus becoming one with the Triple Jewels and all the lineage gurus. True Buddha School's Guru Yoga is a standardized procedure which includes reciting mantras, forming mudras, and doing visualizations.

-H-

Heart Mantra

When a buddha or bodhisattva reaches enlightenment, his enlightenment is mirrored through the frequency of his heart mantra. When one chants the heart mantra, a resonance is created which allows one to merge with that respective buddha or bodhisattva.

Heart Sutra

One of the shortest (260 characters in Chinese) and most famous sutras of the Mahayana Buddhist Sutras. It is based off the *Prajnaparamita Sutra*, which was condensed into the *Diamond Sutra*. Despite its length, it encompasses the Buddhism systemic teachings of existence, emptiness, and realization and can be described as the most profound of all sutras.

-I-

-J-

-K-

Kagyu/ Kagyupa/White Sect

This school became known as the White Sect due to Milarepa, one of the lineage gurus, dressing in a simple white cotton robe when he was in retreat. The sect was founded by lineage gurus beginning with Tilopa to Naropa to Marpa and then to his disciple Milarepa. Nevertheless, it flourished especially during the time of Milarepa's most famous disciple, Gampopa. After Gampopa, it soon fractioned into many sub-sects, known as the Four Great and Eight Minors, headed by Gampopa's chief disciples. It is especially known for its meditation and yogic practices.

Karma (Sanskrit, literally "Action" or "Deed")
The cycle of cause and effect; concept believed amongst the Buddhist, Hindu, Jain and Sikh traditions.

Karmapa (Sanskrit, literally "Buddha-Activity Man")
The spiritual head of the Karma Kagyu Sect of Tibetan Buddhism. The first incarnation of the Karmapa was in 1110 AD, making this the longest lived line of Tibetan Tulkus. Presently, he is in his seventeenth incarnation.

Ksitigarbha Bodhisattva (Sanskrit, literally "Womb of the Earth")
One of the eight mahasattvas (great beings), the bodhisattva of great vows and like all bodhisattvas, he aspires to deliver sentient beings wandering astray in the six realms (hell denizens, hungry ghosts, animals, asuras, humans, and devas), but he specializes in delivering beings from hell. He is usually represented as a standing venerated figure, holding in his right hand a pilgrim's staff, and in his left a pearl. His famous vow is "Not until the hells are emptied will I become a Buddha; not until all beings are saved will I certify to Bodhi."

-L-

Lama
A guru or spiritual teacher in Tibetan Buddhism, who are seen as the embodiment of the Buddha.

Lama Kazi Dawa Samdup (1868-1922 AD)
The head master at Sikkim State Bhutia Boarding School in Gangkok, Lama Kazi Dawa Samdup later served as a translator for the British administration and the Tibetan government. Among his many translations are works such as *The Tibetan Book of the Dead*, *Tibet's Great Yogi Milarepa*, *Shrichakrasambhara Tantra: A Buddhist*

Tantra, An English-Tibetan Dictionary, Tibetan Yoga and Secret Doctrines, and more.

-**M**-

Maha Twin Lotus Ponds
This is the Pure Land of the Padmakumara located in the Western Paradise of the Amitabha. By practicing the True Buddha Tantra, one may travel to the Maha Twin Lotus Ponds in meditation or at the time of death.

Mahasiddha (Sanskrit, literally "Great Adept")
Also known as "tantrikas," these great tantric masters have sufficient accomplishment to be considered gurus and have become the founders of many Buddhist lineage traditions. They come from any social class (kings, priests, yogins, farmers, housewives, prostitutes, etc.), because "ordinary" life and lived experience are held as the principal foundation and sustenance for realization.

Mahasiddhi Saraha
Born circa 8th century AD in Eastern India to a Brahmin family, Mahasiddhi Saraha later studied at the Nalanda University. He is considered to be one of the founders of Vajrayana Buddhism, particularly the Mahamudra tradition.

Mahesvara (Sanskrit, literally "Great Lord of the Universe")
This is another name for Shiva, one of the three main deities of Hinduism. Known also as the Lord of the Yogis, he is typically pictured as blue in color with snakes decorating his body sitting in deep meditation with his trident in the background.

Mandala (Sanskrit, literally "Circle")
It is a symbol which represents the realms of buddhas, bodhisattvas, or dharma protectors. It also represents various energies of particular enlightened states of mind. It may be in two dimensions, as in a painting, or in three dimensions, such as in the placement of sacred objects. The body or even the world at large may be interpreted as a mandala, as they symbolize various aspects of universal energies. The representations are very artistic with intricate colors and designs to aid in visualization. It also refers to a visualization of an offering multiplying infinitely into the space of the entire universe.

Manjushri Bodhisattva (Sanskrit, literally "He Who is Noble and Gentle")
He is the Bodhisattva of Transcendent Wisdom. He is typically depicted with the Prajnaparamita Sutra and a sword which cuts through the clouds of ignorance. His practices may be used to help gain wisdom, knowledge and eloquence.

Mantra
Chants used for blessing, invocation of buddhas, offering, harmonization, purification, protection, longevity, etc.

Mara
Demons or demonic influences which are essentially the same as what is more commonly known as "devil." They manifest in the form of greed, anger, ignorance, jealousy, and other emotions.

Marpa (1012-1097 AD)
Known as the "Great Translator," he travelled from Tibet to India three times to bring back various Tantric Buddhist teachings, especially those of his guru, Naropa.

Meridians
In Traditional Chinese Medicine, these are pathways through which qi flows. In the human body there are approximately 20 meridians which connect the more than 600 acupuncture points. There are "twelve regular meridians" which correspond to each organ.

Milarepa (1025-1135 AD)
After killing his relatives through black magic, he performed hard labor for his guru, Marpa, to remove the negative karma of the black magic. Milarepa practiced the pith instructions accordingly in the high mountains of Tibet, spending twelve years cultivating in the White Horse Tooth Rock Cave. Attaining response though Mahamudra, Milarepa achieved transformation of his supernatural faculties. Among the yoga practitioners of Kagyupa, Milarepa was one of the most famous, most accomplished yogins.

Mingmen
Known as the "Door of Life," this acupressure point is right below the kidneys, exactly opposite to the navel, between the second and third lumbar vertebrae.

Mr. Three-Peaks-Nine-States
Grand Master Lu's first teacher who manifested out of the spiritual realm. He taught Grand Master Lu many spiritual practices, especially those of Taoism.

Mudra
Outward physical expressions of inner states of consciousness. Placing the body in a particular physical position assists one in developing the related inner state. Mudras are typically associated with various hand gestures, but can include other parts of the body.

-N-

Nagas
These serpent-like spiritual beings living in caves, rivers and heavens are known as protectors, benefactors, and a source of wealth. During the Buddha's cultivation of enlightenment, a naga appeared and served the Buddha as a protector from the elements.

Naropa (1016-1100 AD)
A scholar at the famous Nalanda University who left to follow the noted yogi, Tilopa. He is known for the Six Yogas of Naropa which form a major part of the practices of the Tibetan Kagyu School.

Nirmanakaya (Emanation Body)
One of the three dharma bodies, the nirmanakaya body is a physical form of the Buddha in the saha world. For example, Living Buddha Lian-sheng is the nirmanakaya body.

Nirvana (Sanskrit, literally "Cessation")
Cessation of suffering where one is freed from the cycle of rebirth. It is a state where one realizes one's connection with the absolute.

Nyingma/Nyingmapa/Red Sect (Tibetan, literally "School of the Ancients")
This school was founded by Padmasambhava; it is the oldest of the four Tibetan Buddhist schools. It maintains a sophisticated system of study and practice, and its special teaching is Dzogchen.

-O-

-P-

Personal Deity Yoga ("Yidam" in Tibetan)
In this meditation, one merges one's consciousness with a Personal Deity. The Personal Deity represents an enlightened state of consciousness and is chosen to correspond to the basic personality of the practitioner.

Prajnaparamita
The most profound wisdom. It is not the same as knowledge or intelligence, but a more subtle and deeper level of wisdom. This perfect wisdom, or transcendent wisdom, can cross one over from a state of suffering to a state of enlightenment.

Pratyeka-buddha (Solitary Realizer)
A practitioner who attains nirvana without a human teacher, but does not go on to teach others the path towards enlightenment.

-Q-

Qi
Energy which can leak from the mind via craving, greed, anger, ignorance, and wrong views. To cultivate the mind is to cultivate qi, and to cultivate qi is to cultivate the mind.

Qingcheng Sect
This Taoist school is named after Qingcheng Mountain in the western Sichuan Province which was a sacred place of Taoism and kungfu.

-R-

Relic (Sarira)
When a practitioner dies and is cremated, small pearl and jewel like

objects are found in the remaining ashes which may multiply or radiate light.

Reincarnation
In Buddhism, as in Hinduism and various other religions, it is believed that after one dies the spirit enters the bardo realm as it prepares for its next rebirth. One may be reborn in any of the six realms of samsara: hell, heaven, human, animal, asura or hungry ghost. It is also possible for an individual to reincarnate out of samsara and into a pure land, which provides an ideal environment for cultivation and meditation with the intent of reaching enlightenment. An accomplished or realized practitioner (by maintaining conscious awareness during the death process) can choose to return to samsara to continue benefiting sentient beings.

-S-

Sadhana
A means of accomplishment, a sequence of prescribed visualization, mudra, and mantra performed to cut through mental obscuration.

Sakya/Sakyapa/Flower Sect
This sect of buddhism received the name Sakya, meaning "gray earth," due to the color of the ground where the first Sakya monastery was built in central Tibet. It is called the Flower Sect because a flower is the emblem of the family that runs the school. Originally founded by the famous scholar and translator Drokmi Lotsawa in the late eleventh century, it is primarily known for the Lamdre, or the "Path and Its Result," which is a system derived from the *Hevajra Tantra* and which provides a systematic teaching of the entire Buddhist path, including the *Tripitaka* (Vinaya, Sutra, and Abhidharma). This school is especially known for its eminence in scholarship and

Tantric ritual.

Sakya Zhengkong
His Eminence Sakya Zhengkong Rinpoche transmitted the Sakya School's central teaching, Lamdre (The Fruit and its Path), and gave the Acharya Empowerment to Living Buddha Lian-sheng.

Samadhi (Sanskrit, literally "Make firm")
Referring to the state one achieves in meditation where the boundary between the practitioner and the object of the meditation (e.g. the personal deity) vanishes.

Sambhogakaya (Bliss Body)
One of the three dharma bodies, the sambhogakaya is the subtle form of a buddha which usually appears to humans in meditation, visions and dreams. For example, the sambhogakaya of Living Buddha Lian-sheng is known as the White Mahapadmakumara, or Padmakumara.

Samsara (Sanskrit, literally "Journey")
Referring to cyclic existence and the associated sufferings in Buddhist terminology. In Mahayana writings, samara refers to the phenomenal universe and is considered to be the same as nirvana. Although this unity of samsara and nirvana seems contradictory, Mahayana traditions like the Yogacara School teaches that everything is the play of the mind. Hence, samsara and nirvana are just mental labels without any real substances. Therefore, if you ignore the physical aspects of these mental labels and only consider their true nature, samsara and nirvana are one and the same.

Sangha
A Sanskrit word meaning community, assembly, association with

a common goal. In Buddhism it refers to monks (bhikshu) or nuns (bhikshuni) with a higher realization, though in modern times this term has been used to describe groups of Buddhist followers in general. They are responsible for teaching, spreading, translating, and maintaining the teachings of Buddha.

Sanskrit
The language of ancient India. Sanskrit was the language of the Hindu Priest Class and the Veda Scriptures. It was later adopted by Buddhists to record Buddhist scriptures.

Sentient Beings
Broadly speaking, all beings with awareness who have not attained enlighten¬ment and become buddhas. More narrowly, all living beings with awareness within the six realms of reincarnation.

Six Realms
See *Samsara*.

Six Root Senses
Perceptions and discernments of the six sensory organs (six roots) which shape what we perceive reality to be. The six consciousnesses are: (1) sight-consciousness; (2) hearing-consciousness; (3) smell consciousness; (4) taste-consciousness; (5) body-consciousness; (6) thought-consciousness.

Sixteenth Gyalwa Karmapa (August 14, 1924 - November 5, 1981)
Spiritual leader of the Karma Kagyu lineage of Tibetan Buddhism. The first incarnation of the Karmapa was in 1110 AD making this the longest line of Tibetan Tulkus. His Holiness the Sixteenth Gyalwa Karmapa bestowed the highest empowerment of the Five-Buddha Crown Empowerment on Living Buddha Lian-sheng.

Solitary Hearer
See *Sravaka*.

Sravaka (Sanskrit, literally "Hearer")
One who attains liberation being a disciple and hearing the teachings of a buddha.

Subhakarasimha (637-735 AD)
Born as the son of royalty in a northeast Indian kingdom, he turned over his position as king to his oldest brother and entered the monastic life. He studied at Nalanda under Master Dharmagupta, who later instructed Subhakarasimha to become a traveling teacher. Upon arriving to China during the Tang Dynasty, he became well known for his supernatural abilities, and became favored by Emperor Xuanzong. It was during this time that he translated several works of Esoteric Buddhism including the *Mahavairocana Abhisambodhi Tantra*, also known as the *Mahavairocana Sutra*. Subhakarasimha was the first patriarch of the Shingon teachings in China.

Suchness
Known as "tathata" in Sanskrit and Pali, it expresses appreciation of the true nature of reality at any given moment, regardless of the moment being perceived as "good" or "bad." In Zen stories, tathata is often best revealed in the seemingly mundane or meaningless. Shakyamuni Buddha transmitted the awareness of tathata directly to Mahakasyapa in what has come to be rendered in English as the Flower Sermon, where Mahakasyapa simply witnessed the Buddha picking up a flower and then looked at the Buddha and smiled, signifying his direct realization. The Buddha confirmed Mahakasyapa's realization and from this it was shown that enlightenment is attained from direct experience, rather than on rational creeds, doctrinal

scholasticism, intellectualism, and analysis alone.

Suddhavasa Heaven

Also known as the "Pure Abodes," this is a group of five heavens where only non-returners can see and Anagami are reborn.

Sukhavati (Sanskrit, "Western Paradise")

Sukhavati is the Buddha Pure Land founded by the Amitabha Buddha. A realm of consciousness rather than an actual locality, this blissful realm beings may continue striving towards complete enlightenment without the pain and suffering that occurs in the other realms of existence.

Surangama Samadhi (Samadhi of the Heroic Progression)

The *Surangama Samadhi Sutra* describes the powers and abilities which a buddha or tenth level bodhisattva can perform while operating from within this samadhi state, which include: The projection or conjuration of eighty-four thousand other buddhas - identical replicas of himself and equally real; Being able to change sex at will; Placing immense buddha lands into a single pore of the skin; Always presiding over the superknowledges; Always emitting rays of light over all universes without exception; Being able to speak and understand all languages of all universes; Possessing a knowledge which is profound and unfathomable; possessing sovereignty over all the gods and mankind and not becoming proud. A bodhisattva who is immersed in this samadhi also rises beyond birth and death - he appears to die, but he is beyond birth, death and passing on.

In the *Mahaparinirvana Sutra* the Buddha explains this samadhi is the essence of the nature of the Buddha, and is the "mother of all Buddhas." The Buddha also comments that the Surangama Samadhi goes under several other names: Prajnaparamita (Perfect Insight);

Vajra Samadhi (Diamond Samadhi); Simhanada Samadhi (Lion's Roar Samadhi), and Buddhasvabhava (Buddha Essence).

Sutra
Meaning "a thread that keeps things together" in Sanskrit which is the metaphor for a set of rules and principles. In Buddhism, sutras are discourses given by the Shakyamuni Buddha. Its usage has broadened to designate discourses by other buddhas such as the *Mahavairocana Sutra* or other highly regarded sacred Buddhist texts, such as the *Platform Sutra*.

Sutra of the Original Vows of Ksitigarbha Bodhisattva
This sutra recounts how Ksitigarbha became a bodhisattva, his great vow to rescue other sentient beings, and recounts his amazing filial piety in his past lifetimes. The sutra consists of thirteen chapters, divided into three sections.

Sutrayana
"Sutra" refers to teachings of Shakyamuni Buddha which were recorded after his Parinirvana (e.g. *Lotus Sutra, Diamond Sutra, Amitabha Sutra*, etc.) "Yana," means "mode of practice." Therefore, in the Sutrayana traditions, practitioners main method of cultivation is to study, read, print, recite, and propagate the sutras.

-T-

Tao (Dao)
Means "the path to the truth."

Taoism (Daoism)
Focuses on nature, the relationship between humanity and the cosmos, health and longevity, and wu wei (action through inaction),

which is thought to produce harmony with the universe.

Taoist Master Qingzhen
Grand Master Lu met Taoist Master Qingzhen (also known as Reverend Liaoming) while he was residing on Jiji Mountain in Nantou County, Taiwan. Reverend Liaoming was a Vajrayana Master and a Fourteenth Generation Disciple of the Qingcheng Taoist School.

Tathagata (Sanskrit, literally "Thus Come One")
A synonym for "Buddha," it refers to the primordially pure Buddha-nature which can neither be created anew nor ever destroyed. This nature can remain obscured indefinitely if not purified and developed.

Ten Directions
This refers to the spatial directions east, southeast, south, southwest, west, northwest, north, northeast, the nadir, and the zenith. Essentially, it means anywhere.

Three Realms
The Desire Realm, Form Realm, and Formless Realm. It is another way in which Buddhism distinguishes between different modes of existence. The Desire Realm encompasses the hell realm, animal realm, human realm, asura realm, and heavens up to the Parmanirmitavasavartin Heavens. The common characteristic is that the beings in this realm are dominated by desire. The Form Realm encompasses the four dhyani heavens. The beings in this realm have renounced desire but they still have not renounced form. So, the beings in these heavens still have form and reside in celestial palaces. The Formless Realm encompasses the four formless heavens. The beings in this realm have renounced both desire and form to exist in states of formlessness.

Three Times
Referring to the past, present, and future.

Thusness
See *Suchness*.

Tientai School (Heavenly Terrace Mountain Sect)
It is one of the ten major schools of Chinese Buddhism primarily based on the *Lotus Sutra*. The first patriarch, Huiwen (550-577 AD) founded the school. The third patriarch, Zhiyi (531-597 AD) established this Mahayana school on the Tian Tai Mountain during the Sui Dynasty. He taught the rapid attainment of Buddhahood through the practice of observing the mind and emphasized both scriptural study and practice.

Tilopa (988–1069 AD)
Born into the to a royal brahmin family in India, Guru Tilopa later adopted a monastic life. Then, upon receiving orders from a dakini, he adopted the life of a wandering mendicant. He began to travel throughout India, receiving teachings from many human gurus. From Nagajuna he received the teachings of the Radiant Light, Illusory Body, *Chakrasamvara Tantra*, and the *Lagusamvara Tantra*. From from Saryapa he learned tummo (inner heat), from Lawapa Dream Yoga, from Sudhasiddhi Bardo, from Indrabhuti Prajna, and from Matangi how to resurect the dead.

Tilopa also received teachings on the entirety of Mahamudra directly from Buddha Vajradhara. He then became a wandering practitioner and after teaching Naropa, appointed him as his successor. Tilopa gave Naropa a teaching called the Six Words of Advice: 1) mi mno (Don't recall – let go of what has passed); 2) mi bsam (Don't imagine - let go of what may come); 3) mi shes (Don't think - let go of what is happening now); 4) mi dpyod (Don't examine - don't try to figure anything out); 5) mi sgom (Don't control - don't try to make anything happen); 6) rang sar bzhag (Rest - relax right now and rest).

Tripitaka
Referred to as the "Three Baskets" since these early writings were made on long, narrow leaves, which were sewn together on one side and then stored in baskets, these writings contain the teachings of Shakyamuni Buddha. The texts are divided into three sections: the Sutras (the Buddha's sermons), Vinaya (precepts/discipline), and Abhidharma (higher level teachings). It is debated if the texts were recorded during the First Council immediately after the Buddha's Parinirvana, or in later centuries. Theraveda Buddhism uses the Tripitaka as the sole canonical text, whereas Vajrayana Buddhism also relies heavily on the tantras for teachings (e.g. *Hevajra Tantra*, *Kalchakra Tantra*, etc.).

Triple Jewels (Triple Gems)
The three precious entities of Buddhism in which all Buddhists take refuge in; they are the Buddha, Dharma, and Sangha.

True Buddha School
In 1975, Living Buddha Lian-sheng established Ling Xian Zong in Taiwan and he officially changed its name to True Buddha School on March 1, 1983. In 1985 Living Buddha Lian-sheng established the main True Buddha School temple, the Ling Shen Ching Tze Temple in Seattle, which was dedicated to the propagation of the True Buddha Tantra.

Tushita Heaven
One of the heavens of Kamadhatu (the Realm of Desire), this heaven is located between the Yama heaven and the Nirmanarati heaven.

This is where the future buddha, Maitreya Buddha, currently resides.

-U-

-V-

Vajra (dorje) (Sanskrit, literally "Diamond Scepter")
A common ritual object in Vajrayana Buddhist practices which represents a thunderbolt, or diamond, which in turn represent being indestructible. It can symbolize the male aspect of enlightenment (skillful means), whereas the vajra bell represents the feminine aspect of enlightenment (wisdom).

Vajrabodhi (671-741AD)
Born to and Indian brahmin family, Vajrabodhi became a monk at a young age. During his travels to Sri Lanka and Sumatra he met his teacher Nagabodhi. After immigrating to China, Vajrabodhi translated many texts from Sanskrit to Chinese, one of the most famous being the partial translation of *Sarvatathāgatatattvasagraha*. His most famous student was Amoghavajra.

Vajradhara (Sanskrit, literally "Thunderbolt-bearer")
Symbolizes the Primordial Buddha. He is typically represented as sitting in the lotus position with his arms crossed on his breast and his hands holding the bell and vajra.

Vajraraja
Sanskrit term for Mantra Kings, Wisdom Kings, Knowledge Kings, or Kings of Light. It may also refer to a dharma protector.

Vajrasattva Practice (Vajrasattva Hundred-Syllable Mantra Practice)
Major deity of Vajrayana Buddhism, by chanting the Hundred Syl-

lable Mantra of Vajrasattva, one is able to quickly remove negative karma. Recitation the Hundred Syllable Mantra one hundred thousand times is one of the Four Preliminary Practices.

Vajrayana Buddhism (Sanskrit, literally "Diamond Vehicle") Also known as the Vehicle of Indestructible Reality and Secret Mantrayana ("Mantra Vehicle"), is a form of Mahayana Buddhism in which the guru teaches an accelerated path to enlightenment through the practices of the three secrets of speech (chanting mantras), body (forming mudras), and mind (visualization). There is a vital element of the teacher-student relationship. The respect of the teacher is extremely vital in Vajrayana because the teacher is the living embodiment of the Three Jewels of the Buddha, Dharma, and Sangha.

Among its many names, this system is called the secret mantra because the profound three secrets of the buddha (enlightened body, speech, and mind) are taught as the innate nature of all phenomena. However, this profound truth is concealed by the beginningless delusion which has obscured the minds of sentient beings and must be revealed skillfully. It is taught in secret and not shown to practitioners with mundane aspirations. It is called mantra because the three secrets are presented as it actually is which is beyond the perceptions of ordinary mind.

The Vajrayana trainings consist of two phases. In the first phase is the "generation stage." These teachings emphasize on the three secrets of the tathagatas, removing trainee's obscuration to recognize that one's own body, speech, and mind are the same as that of the enlightened body, speech, and mind of a buddha. In the second phase, the "perfection stage," the trainee learns to direct the subtle vital energy and essence within the body's energy channels to manifest great bliss, inner radiance, and emptiness. Through this experiential sequence, the obscurations of trainee are removed to recognize the innate awareness that has always been there. Through the diligent practice of Vajrayana teachings, one may dissolve the beginningless delusion and attain buddhahood within a single lifetime.

-W-

White Padmakumara (Sanskrit, literally "Lotus Youth")
The sambhogakaya (bliss body) form of Living Buddha Lian-sheng, a great fortune-bestowing and hindrance removing bodhisattva. For more details about Padmakumara and his abode, the Maha Twin Lotus Ponds in the Western Paradise, see the *True Buddha Sutra*.

-X-

-Y-

Yamantaka Practice
The merits of this practice are enormous, because the Lord of Death (Lord Yama) was conquered by Yamantaka and became his subordinate. If one practices his sadhana, one can gain mastery over ones life and death, and can live to an old age.

Yin and Yang
An ancient Chinese philosophy which explains how our universe is. It is the basis of Chinese medicine, martial arts, divination techniques, and Taoism. Yin refers feminine, cold, and dark. Yang is masculine, hot, and light. They are polar opposites, neither good nor bad, which come together to create balance.

Yoga (Sanskrit, literally "Union")
In Buddhism, it is a method uniting an individual self with the Buddha. It includes physical and mental exercises which help one reach enlightenment.

Yogi (Yogin)
Commonly referring to one who intensely practices meditation and rituals. A female is known as a yogini.

Yogic Response (Spiritual Response)
By practicing mudras, mantras and visualizations the respective deity invoked and the practitioner is at an equal level with the Three Secrets (body, speech, and mind) of the Tathagata, and thus possesses limitless meritorious functions. Once the practitioner merges with the principal deity, he or she gains access into the dharma realm through this single gateway.

-Z-

Zen Patriarch
A major lineage master of Zen Buddhism. It is most often used to refer to the Zen or Chan Patriarchs in China, from Bodhidharma to Huineng.

Also From **US Daden Culture**

Sheng-yen Lu Book Collection 163:
Crossing the Ocean of Life and Death
Sale Price: $12.00 USD
ISBN-13: 978-0-9841561-0-0
ISBN-10: 0-9841561-0-0

Sheng-yen Lu Book Collection 148:
The Power of Mantra
Sale Price: $12.00 USD
ISBN-13: 978-0-9841561-1-5
ISBN-10: 0-9841561-1-9

Sheng-yen Lu Book Collection 154:
The Aura of Wisdom
Sale Price: US $12.00 dollars

ISBN-13: 978-0-9841561-4-6
ISBN-10: 0-9841561-4-3

3440 Foothill Blvd. • Oakland, CA 94601 • U.S.A. • www.usdaden.com

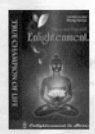